Come Out

of

Hiding

and

SHINE

An Anthology

Compiled by Rebecca Hall Gruyter

Come Out of Hiding and Shine
Compiled by Rebecca Hall Gruyter

© September 2016

Published by *Believe In Your Dreams Publishing*

Acknowledgments

On the behalf of Believe in Your Dreams Publishing, we would like to express an abundance of gratitude and love to Rebecca Hall Gruyter (The Purpose Driven Leader) for trusting the Believe in Your Dreams Publishing team with your amazing project. This is only the beginning of the greatness we will spread over this amazing world together.

Believe in Your Dreams Publishing would like to extend further appreciation and gratitude to every co-author who shared their stories. These stories will touch and, hopefully, transform the lives of so many people across this great nation. Thanks for BELIEVING in me and my rocking team. We love you all.

~ **Nichole Peters**

Table of Contents

Section 4: Your Time is Now!

Section 5: The Choice is Yours: Choose to SHINE!

Foreword

"Come Out of Hiding and SHINE!"
Rebecca Hall Gruyter

Thank you for leaning into *Come Out of Hiding and SHINE*! I'm honored and excited to bring this powerful book to you, featuring thirty experts who are committed to helping you SHINE powerfully in your life!

As a women's empowerment leader, I know a lot about being disempowered and how to overcome that to step into your power and into the center stage of your life and SHINE! It is a courageous act to say yes to you and be willing to let others walk beside you to support and cheer you on in life.

I was honored when Nichole Peters from Believe In Your Dreams Publishing wanted to publish a book for me and then leaned in to the heart and vision of thirty experts sharing their hearts, wisdom, and how to *Come Out of Hiding and SHINE*. In sharing their stories, they will equip and empower you to tap into your truth and SHINE. I believe this book is a living and interactive book that will speak wisdom, motivation, encouragement, and power into your life. Your heart will be touched and you will be motivated and inspired to take action to step forward powerfully in your life. I want to invite you to pause, take a deep breath, and be ready to receive these powerful stories and messages so they can ignite a fire, courage, and purpose in your life to inspire you to take more action and SHINE!

The reason I'm so passionate about women stepping forward and sharing their wisdom, heart, lives, and stories is because I came from a very disempowered place. I experienced all types of abuse from the tender ages of five until thirteen years old (my formative years). I actually continued to visit that abusive environment until the age of eighteen. This environment of abuse taught me that "I am not okay", there is "something wrong with me", that it must be "my fault," and that it is "NOT safe to be seen or heard". I was an expert in hiding. When I was finally rescued by my birth father and placed in his home with my stepmother, who became the mother of my heart, I got to start my healing journey.

On this journey, I discovered that these false beliefs I had from before were actually lies. I discovered that I am beautifully and wonderfully made (just like you), on purpose and for a purpose; that I matter and am needed just as I am; that it wasn't my fault; and ultimately that it is safe to be seen, heard, and SHINE! So my mission, the calling of my heart, is to help others understand these truths: that we are all beautifully and wonderfully made and needed just as we are. When we step forward and share the gift of us, it makes a difference in our lives and in the lives of those around us. This means we have to be willing to be seen on the same level that we are wanting to serve and make a difference in the world. The more you SHINE, the more you are paving the way for others while sharing the amazing gift of you with the world.

My heart's desire and calling is to equip and empower women to step into the center of their life - not just life as a supporting character or a role of some sort, but to really step forward fully in your life. Bring it all; authentically and powerfully share your story, life, and heart with others. Some of the greatest gifts I have been given are by women who invested their life and heart in me. Pattie (my stepmother), the mom of my heart, used to let me follow her around everywhere and she invested her heart and life in me. We built beautiful memories and moments together because she leaned into me; and opened her heart and life to me, showing me how a mother's heart can love and not hurt; but heal, hold, celebrate, and inspire.

I also have been blessed by my grandmothers (all four of them) who chose to invest their lives in me too. They shared their wisdom, love, life lessons, and beautiful traditions, leaving a legacy of strength, character, and loving messages that have healed, encouraged, and lifted up thousands of women throughout the years. They created the roots I now stand on, roots that go deep, weather storms, and go deep enough and are strong enough to sustain the path I'm called to walk. I discovered life is not a solo journey. We each need other to encourage us, to speak wisdom and truth into us, to love us and cheer us on, and to help us stand up again when we fall. This book will walk beside you to help you run and not grow weary, to complete all that you are called to complete, and to SHINE in your life and business!

I asked each heart-centered and powerful co-author to share some of their personal story and journey with you. As they share from their respective journeys with you, they share what they have learned, their wisdom, and what they wish someone had encouraged them with or whispered in their ear...especially in those dark and challenging times. They are committed to pouring into you, to equip and empower you in your life. Throughout the chapters you will feel a consistent and transparent heartbeat to support you in very real ways as the authors often share what they wish they would have known. We want to make your path and journey easier for you as you step forward to coming out of hiding and SHINE! As the book compiler, I'm so proud of what each co-author has shared in their chapters, and am honored to have each of them leaning in to support you. I am equally honored that you have said yes to our book and are entrusting us to support you on your journey.

Now it's your turn. Are you going to lean in and learn from the wisdom within this book? Will you let us walk beside you on your journey of life? We want to lift you up, support you, encourage, and empower you. It is your choice. We want to help you grow deep roots that can weather the storms in life. You can choose to open the pages and let them pour into you, or you can put it on a shelf. My heart and prayer is that you will say yes to you and lean into the powerful messages and hope that are waiting to pour into you, your heart, and your life.

You all have unique gifts, talents, abilities, stories, journeys, and perspectives that you alone can bring forward. Those in your life need you, your message, your wisdom, your perspective, gifts, talents, and heart. You are a beautiful flower in the garden of life with your own fragrance, color, style, season, texture, and beauty that only you can bring forward. When we shrink back or hide, the garden becomes less vibrant and we all miss out. Be willing to share the gift of you with those around you and with the world! Be willing to be seen on the same level you are willing/wanting to serve.

Here is how to get the most out of this powerful book. It is divided it into five sections, each one designed to meet you exactly where you are at and to support you real time in your journey of coming out of hiding to SHINE: "Yes, You Can!"; "You are Beautifully and Wonderfully Made"; "You ARE Enough!"; "Your Time is Now!"; and "The Choice is Yours, Choose to SHINE!" I encourage you to pick the section that pulls at your heart the most each time you pick up the book and then select one or two chapters in that section to support you with the focus that will be of the greatest support you to each time you open this dynamic book. You will find, at the end of each chapter, the contact information and a little bit about each author. I know that they would love to hear from you, to know how their chapter supported you, and they would love to build a connection with your through social media, etc. I encourage you to Friend and follow those authors that feel a powerful resonance and connection with so that they can continue to pour into and support you on your journey in life.

Now the next step is yours. Drink in the stories and messages that are within its pages to serve, support, and inspire you. Take the time to pause, read, and reflect. Listen to the powerful messages and hope that are waiting for you within its powerful pages. It's not an accident that you purchased this book and are opening it to read right now...today. I invite you to lean in and truly receive the messages and wisdom that will speak to your heart and soul that you will find in these transformational and dynamic pages. Enjoy this rich collection of wisdom, love, and encouragement so that you can go forth in life, Come Out of Hiding and SHINE!

~Rebecca Hall Gruyter, Book Compiler

Biography

Rebecca Hall Gruyter is the owner of Your Purpose Driven Practice, CEO of RHG Media Productions, creator of the Women's Empowerment Series events/TV show, the Speaker Talent Search™, and Rebecca's Money Summit. Rebecca is the Network Director for VoiceAmerica's Women Channel in both radio and TV, is an in-demand speaker, an expert money coach, and a frequent guest expert on success panels, tele-summits, TV, and radio shows.

As the CEO of RHG Media Productions™, Rebecca launched the international #1 TV channel called Empowered ConnectionsTV™ on the VoiceAmerica TV Network, bringing transformational TV shows and programming to the world. In January 2017, she is launching her new TV Network to bring even more positive and transformational programming to the world. She is a popular and syndicated radio talk show host and #1 bestselling author (multiple times) who wants to help YOU impact the world powerfully!

Learn More...

(925) 787-1572

www.YourPurposeDrivenPractice.com

www.EmpoweredConnectionsTV.com

www.EmpoweringWomenTransformingLives.com

www.MeetWithRebecca.com

https://www.youtube.com/channel/UCtxW8aE4_csCNreslTzxwmQ

Section 1: Yes You Can!

In this heart-centered section you will hear stories of amazing experts that will encourage, inspire and remind you that you, absolutely can come of hiding and SHINE! Enjoy this powerful set of inspirational stories, truths, and powerful actions you can take to help you believe you can too! We believe in you and can't wait to see you come out of hiding and SHINE!

Warmly,

Rebecca Hall Gruyter, Book Compiler and Empowerment Leader

Divine Messages
Kathleen E. Sims

I remember walking into my first grade classroom to find this loving woman teacher. She was so different than my emotionally distant mother. I vividly recall thinking, "When I grow up, I'm going to be a teacher and mother just like her."

In the eighth grade, when I was coming home from another unfulfilling counseling session, I was commiserating to myself how much I didn't like going. The counselor I went to wouldn't say a word. She waited in silence until I got so uncomfortable and started nervously chatting. Supposedly she was counseling me to be safe from my violent father. After a few sessions I was on the bus going home and I thought, "When I grow up, I am going to be a counselor, and unlike the one I am going to, I'll help adults learn how to be better parents so children don't suffer from harm done the way I have."

I've heard it said that we are often "naturally" guided to a lifework that is a reflection of something we are trying to make "right" from our childhoods. My journey is the perfect example, guided from *Divine Messages* in many forms.

I held tightly onto both those determined decisions about my future. I would go to college and become a teacher and counselor. However, when I was sixteen years old, my path took a very divergent turn. The universe seemed to have something else in store for me. I was sitting in the high school cafeteria with my girlfriend when two guys walked in. They caught my attention immediately. I asked my friend if she knew the one in the suit and she said, "No."

"I'm going to go out with him," I heard myself say. I didn't recognize these words as my own. A moment later, a vivid picture came into my mind and engulfed me. I saw myself married to the dark-haired guy, living in suburbia with two kids, a dog, and a house with a white picket fence. Not only did I see this, I *felt* it, as surely as if it had already happened. Linear time had disappeared, and in that moment, I was living the future.

"Actually," I blurted out, "I'm going to marry him."

Needless to say, my friend was speechless. Looking back, I can hardly believe it myself. But after that day, I committed to this vision of my future with bold behavior and confidence to match. I got his friend to set us up on a first date. He didn't have a chance - not that he wanted one.

And the rest, as they say, is history.

A year later, Jim and I were married and soon we had a baby on the way. We'd already purchased our own home, complete with a white picket fence. I wasn't even eighteen years old yet. Everyone told us, "It won't last; you're too young." But I already knew how things would turn out: four decades of deep, abiding, soulmate love.

The knowledge had been bestowed upon me by something greater than myself, from "On High" through a *Divine Clairvoyant Vision.*

I loved being a devoted wife and mother. However, I had given up my childhood dream. College was not in the cards. I was happy about my choice, yet never forgot the earlier yearnings to impact people's lives.

When my girls became teenagers, it seemed they no longer needed much attention. I started becoming restless and was drawn to the human potential movement. While I was sitting in a room of 200 people in a very powerful four-day workshop, my childhood dreams started resurrecting, flooding back into my mind, and I heard another significant *Divine Message* in my head: "You <u>can</u> do it! And you can do it <u>your way</u>!"

I didn't know what that meant nor what to do about it. My restlessness and lack of knowing how to make my dreams come true became low-key depression.

My older daughter was growing impatient with me and one day screamed, "Get a life! You're playing small, pretending you're just a suburban housewife. We have fun things we want to do with our friends after school and we don't want to come home early because you're waiting for us. You're a powerful person hiding behind all that weight, hoping no one will notice. I love you and that's why I'm telling you this, and I'm not going to stop until you realize it's the truth!"

I was stunned and I felt a desperate need to defend myself. "Don't you love me the way I am? Don't you like the life we created for you kids? Leave me alone!"

Then it happened – I felt like my brain was lasered open and I saw the vivid truth. I am a powerful person with a lot to give the world, but because I hate rejection, I had operated in life with a "don't notice me" attitude, quietly going about my accomplishments and avoiding detection.

In that moment, I realized it was TRUE! I was protecting myself by playing small in the world, and hiding behind an extra forty pounds, hoping no one would expect much from me. It hit me like a ton of bricks that I was doing this unconsciously on purpose.

Another poignant *Divine Message* - this time delivered through my daughter – but I didn't yet recognize it as such.

With this new, deeply felt truth, I knew I was caught and that I couldn't deny my personal power and capabilities again. I had to be willing to go from being invisible to being seen...to *Come Out of Hiding and Shine!* I knew that a miracle beyond my understanding had happened to me on an internal level, and there was no going back into my "small self."

Now what? I was totally silent for three days, adjusting internally to this new sense of Self. I had no idea what to do with my new identity and Self-recognition, but something inside me certainly knew. Weight began to melt away and I magically lost forty pounds without dieting in the next eight weeks. I realized the principles I had learned in a seminar about how to be a naturally thin person had kicked in effortlessly. I saw that my limiting beliefs about who I was were false illusions and they started falling away. I willingly acknowledged my God-given gifts, and another *Divine Message* came: "You have to follow your lifelong calling.

Within four months I was working for a transformational seminar company - being trained on the job to be a seminar leader and counselor. My childhood dream came true. I did do it - and I did it my way! I loved my job. I had the privilege of empowering women to experience their own authentic selves and express that in the world, as I was finally doing!

I had my dream job for ten wonderful years, with profound experiences under my belt. I traveled around the country teaching transformational Personal Power Seminars to thousands of women, training other trainers, and serving on the company's management team. It was very fulfilling: miracles, abundance, and the experience of making a true contribution.

The company's owner suddenly changed her belief system and wanted to rewrite all of our seminars to fit her new view on life. Then, in an instant, she made a major management change and the rug was being pulled out from under me. Poof! My dream job was gone. It was shocking how quickly it all disappeared.

I was devastated that I had lost it all, and even more importantly, at how my personal power and identity left with it. All I knew to do was go home to bed and hide for months. Then I thought that surely I could use the Empowerment Principles I'd been teaching for the past ten years to get myself out of bed and engaged in life again!

Okay! Okay! I started to pray without ceasing: "Please God, use me. Show me the way. What do I do? Where can I make the best contribution?"

Another few weeks went by...then it happened again!

In a flash, the heavens opened up and I got another life-changing *Divine Message* – this time as a vision. I saw a picture with a message for me that was astonishingly profound. It was the earth completely surrounded with triangles of light – and that light was radiating everywhere. Each point of light represented a person connected to others in triangles all around the planet like a grid. I saw the way everything in the universe worked in perfect Divine Order. There was a place for everyone to share the gifts they'd been given from On High fulfilling every need on the planet: harmony, peace, and love prevailed.

I heard the voice of the Divine say, *"This is the perfection of the Divine Plan made manifest. Everyone has an essential part and contribution to the whole. That also means you!"*

I got out my journal and began to write the *Divine Messages* that came through as fast as I could. *"These are the steps people must go through to realize at a cellular level this same Divine Truth for themselves."* I looked at what had been written. It was a three-day Spiritual Intensive.

Every cell of my Being was vibrating at a speed I wasn't accustomed to. I read everything I wrote and sobbed. I knew I was not the same person who had been lying there for so many excruciating months.

I realized that my True Identity wasn't dependent on my life situation. Instead, I saw that I am an evolving Being, unfolding more of my authentic self with each phase of my awakening.

"Now what? No one will hire me to do this!" I thought. "And I don't want to start my own business. So what on earth am I supposed to do with these insights and workshop?"

Another *Divine Directive* came: "Get out of bed and talk to anyone who will listen. Share your Vision."

I followed the instructions, opened my heart, and began sharing my profound insights about these principles and Divine Truths.

Before I knew it, a business had organically taken form around me. I was teaching "Live Your Vision Consulting System" in businesses, transforming cultures, and offering the "Live Your Vision" weekend workshop to the general public, transforming individual's lives as well. I was aligned with my true calling - expressing the gifts that had been bestowed upon me and fulfilling my unique Divine Blueprint. It inspired me and restored my faith. I saw thousands of people awaken to their Life Purpose and discover their unique part in the Divine Plan.

Your *Divine Messages* are waiting to be bestowed upon you. You, too, are essential to God's plan to awaken humanity!

Ask yourself:

Does my inner dialogue keep me "small", or empower the expression of my authentic self to unfold?

What *Divine Messages* have I gotten in my life? Did I act on them or override them?

Who am I?

Why am I here?

How can I be of the highest service?

What is my unique place in this world?

Then:

Meditate and journal. Don't think about it. Allow your answers to come through you from something higher than your own mind.

Be part of the solution to global awakening! Find your true path. Express your unique and essential part in God's plan. Let's together birth a new humanity.

Join me in my stand:

One million people will know and be living their Life Purpose!

My Gift to you: a recorded Teleclass, *Discovering Your Life Purpose in 1 Hour*. You will create a statement of your Life Purpose and gain knowledge on how to use it as a lifelong guidance tool.

Pass it forward...

Ask others to join you on your journey of purposeful living!

Biography

Kathleen E. Sims, D.D., C.H.T., is co-founder of The Center for Conscious Living in Pleasant Hill, CA and the creator of the educational website www.kathleenthelovecoach.com. Serving singles, couples, and families globally, she brings her "body of work" forth in many forms: soul-based counseling, spiritual healing, hypnotherapy, life and love coaching, and transformational workshops. In person or online, one can access her powerful Love Teachings worldwide through Skype and her Teleseminars and group coaching programs. Her work is mystical, yet practical, based on Universal Spiritual Principles and Transformational Coaching Technologies, resulting in permanent change where all things become possible.

After manifesting her life partner and soulmate at the age of sixteen they grew, evolving their relationship into conscious and mature, deep love, lasting four decades. After Jim's sudden transition, she attracted a second amazing soulmate at the age of sixty-one. Kathleen is gifted with the unique ability to draw from deep personal experiences, translating them into The Legacy of Love Teachings so others can attract deep abiding love.

Kathleen has an uncanny ability to recognize soulmate partnerships, thus bringing her the joy of officiating at many clients' weddings. It fulfills her to see their happy faces and know they learned to attract, enhance, and maintain a deep connection and true unconditional love.

Teaching love as her life service, she started a movement - The Self Love Revolution, in which to "begin your journey to the heart" – at the live event, The Love Shop. She has dedicated her life to healing the world by spreading love one heart at a time.

She is the co-author of four personal growth books that have hit #1 on the bestseller list. In her soon-to-be released *Evolutionary Love - The Secret to Finding True Love and a Lasting Relationship,* she will reveal her proven system of clearing the portal through which a soulmate can be attracted and one's Divine Blueprint expressed.

A sought-after featured speaker at conferences and gatherings and radio host of "The New You", she has been interviewed on Voice America Radio and TV, sharing her inspiring love story. She has been the featured Love Coach on Selfgrowth.com and on Arielle Ford's Soulmate Secrets' site. She has her own YouTube channel with many educational videos to help bring more love into the world.

She is a graduate of the University of Science and Philosophy and a certified Life and Relationship Coach from J.F.K. University, utilizing many certified Healing Modalities. She sees herself as a change agent for the transformation of the global family. Her vision is that every person whose heart innately yearns for a loving, fulfilling relationship has one, and it is expressed in the world through love and light - *for in the presence of love, all are touched.*

Learn More...

www.Kathleenthelovecoach.com

www.facebook.com/kathleenthelovecoach/

www.facebook.com/kathleen.e.sims

www.linkedin.com/in/kathleen-e-sims

Get Out of the Darkness and Rock Your SHINE Power!
Nichole Peters

Hidden in the Darkness that Rises

I grew up in Bogalusa, Louisiana, in the Redmond Heights Projects, one of the most downtrodden and impoverished areas of my hometown. Right now, in my small city, there is still active segregation. You can find a black YMCA and white YMCA or a white cemetery and black cemetery in different parts of town. When I attended BHS there was a separate prom for black and white folks.

I grew up surrounded by oppression, even in the black community, because my chocolate skin color wasn't considered beautiful, and quite a few looked down on me. It didn't help that my father lived a double life, so I suffered as a child conceived in bigamy.

I was told by my elementary teacher that my dream, which was to become a successful author, was doomed because writing and reading comprehension were my weakest areas. After I graduated high school, I lost my father and my grandmother less than one year apart and in my grief, I got involved with a notorious drug dealer. I ended up flunking out of college twice!

As a barely grown adult, I was constantly fighting the man who was supposed to love me. After giving birth to four children I went from a perfect size 8 to a whooping 3XL. Three of my children were born premature and with challenges. Stress and depression took control. People laughed at the way I spoke and assumed I was ignorant. They believed that my voice was loud because I was oblivious. Little did they know that because of abuse, I could barely hear out of my left ear. Later, I was forced to learn how to control the tone and the volume of my voice.

Many people overlooked my worth. My own self-value was extremely low. I felt let down by family, school, society, and even God! I was a nobody, another statistic, so I ran to the streets. For a short time, I seemed to have value living a hardcore lifestyle. I thrived in a criminal setting surrounded by the "wrong crowd" while the good girl inside lay hidden, trapped within chains fashioned from negativity. I developed an "I don't give a damn" attitude that set me on a path of darkness. Eventually, deadened inside, I became suicidal. I beat myself up over my past mistakes. An overwhelming wave of dispiriting dark thoughts led me to think I would never SHINE, so I hid in the darkness.

Reinvention of Darkness through Prayer

Have you ever suffered agony to the point that you were just ready to DIE, tired of being tired and sick? I needed to escape the lifestyle that had, at first, made me feel special, but eventually led to inner conflict and pain. Eventually I attempted to leave the darkness that had me enveloped in its shadow. I did not want my children raised in the ferocity element. I started going back to church. I sang praises to the heavens and studied the Bible. However, the darkness didn't want to let me go. It attacked me with sickness, the physical abuse got worse, and the only time I got respite was when I stopped praying. The darkness had grown strong and I paid a huge price for worshipping God. The better I did for myself and loved ones, the more pain I felt. I witnessed more suffering. I threw my hands up and gave into darkness because of fear. Vast mistake!

Eventually, all that controlled my mindset were unwanted thoughts. I accepted that I was a complete loser, a defeated, unworthy soul, destined to fail for the rest of my life. In my weakness, I accepted the spiritual darkness as my due. I deserved pain and punishment. The darkness clouded my mind, body, and spirit, leaving me brokenhearted and alone.

I will never forget the day that I literally ran towards death, from the living room and down the hallway to my Ma'Dear's bedroom. I opened all her drawers, looking for her pistol, but her gun was no longer there. After fully searching her bedroom, I chose another way. I decided to overdose on some of my prescription pills. I chose the bathtub as the best place to sacrifice my life. I loved to praise and worship in the tub and, for some odd reason, I felt God would forgive and accept me into Heaven if I killed myself in that tub, since He knew my pain more than anybody.

I sat there, soaking in both water and tears, before grabbing two pill bottles and a cup of orange juice. I twisted off the caps and was ready to pour out a fatal handful of pills, but something whispered *"try to pray first."* I wanted to protest because every time I'd tried to pray, I just couldn't get it right, but the voice sounded like my granny. Her angel's voice convinced me to shift in that tub until I was on my knees. I pleaded my case to Father God. I prayed so hard that I literally started speaking in another tongue. My bath water cooled and changed color. It looked like milk and honey. I was in pain but I couldn't stop praying and praising the **LOVE** of God. My bath towel turned into a microphone. My mirror became my congregation and my reinforced voice became the guide and **POWER** I needed to heal. I urged myself to **RESPECT** life's blessings. I needed to live, to shine, and give all my darkness to the Lord. I had found my inner strength! I started praise dancing and shouting until both bottles were knocked over and pills spilled all over the floor. I knew then there was a God!

That night I promised God that no matter what I went through, I would never give up. He gave me a new voice so that I could do good for others. As a result, I promised I would never try to take myself out. Read

Isaiah 60:1-5 and you will understand like I do that NO darkness would ever hide my glorious light ever again.

My Moment to Welcome in the Shine

Even though I had to depend on public assistance to carry me through the process of escaping poverty, I still had faith and kept going. In 2005, I witnessed the worst storm in America's history. Hurricane Katrina stormed though my hometown, leaving us with very little food and no power or clean water for weeks. I was nearly eight months pregnant with my fourth child and had just been released from the hospital in New Orleans after having severe complications, but God was with me. FEMA gave people the option to relocate to different states. I decided to take the opportunity. Change was needed in my life and moving away from the bad elements I was trying to avoid would give me full responsibility for my life.

I will never forget the day I packed up the U-Haul and left. I turned back around and gave my Ma'Dear a hug and kiss. I whispered in her ear with tears rolling down my face, *"I am going to welcome the light that wants to shine in my life."*

Ma'Dear grabbed my face and said, "Go get 'em, Nikki Pooh."

Five years later, in 2010, I formed an organization called Women of Love, Power, and Respect. The organization was set up to help women who were trapped in bondage to break every chain. I booked speaking engagements and held social media events all over world to share the good news. In 2011, I unleashed my inner warrior even further and faced my fears. I decided to pursue my adolescent dream to write books. My first book was titled *A Woman of Love, Power, and Respect.* After publications issues, I decided to publish my own work and name it "Believe in Your Dreams Publishing."

I wanted to show my children and others who believed they couldn't succeed that no matter what obstacles you face in life, you should never stop believing in yourself or your dreams!

Shine Bright Like a Diamond and Warrior Up!

My struggle was uncommonly hard because the darkness didn't want me to find my voice. I was blind and didn't realize that I was a valuable, powerful, and beautiful person. The last decade has been a journey in which I've realized I am a unique Warrior with a mission to fight hard for others. I was destined to raise above all the hidden pain. After praying in that bathtub, Father God delivered a powerful message: stand tall and go forth with His creation. My Father assured me that I was his. "Ye are of God, little children, and have overcome them: because greater is he that is in you, than he that is in the world." *1 John 4:4.*

My grandmother and Ma'Dear always told me I was cut from a different cloth - a worthy creation. You must realize you are valuable too! There will always be sour lemon juice squeezed at us, but we must have hope that God will connect us to our purpose, then sweeten our lives. Believe in His power and become your greatest ally by releasing your inner warrior. Drink a glass of lemonade and shine!

Spiritually: Stay spiritually connected in order to shine through your darkest hours. I had to let go of anything that interrupted my purpose journey. I had to learn to FIGHT, seek light, and live a cheerful lifestyle. Darkness can't resist trying to hide light and will come for you, but confront the challenge. Give the darkness nothing and give light everything. Pray and meditate always!

Mentally: Your mindset has everything to do with how you perform daily. Embrace change and open up your mind to welcome positive thinking, self-love, and hope. It's important to stand up for sanity and set up a powerful mindset that shows your worth.

Emotionally: Emotions can make or break you. However, you must understand that they are not never meant to control over your mind nor your life. You hold the power by governing anger that turns into rage or sadness that turns into depression. This can send you into a delusional state. Enough is enough! Snatch your happiness and power back!

Physically: I was diagnosed with over seven illnesses and was taking fourteen medications. I suffered major setbacks and was unable to finish my books or speaking events. I knew I had to fight for a healthier life. I refused to lose my health after winning over the darkness, so God led me down a holistic healing path. I'm now on just four medications daily.

Believe in yourself!

I am now an internationally recognized motivational speaker, bestselling author, publisher, and TV/Radio host. I choose to shine by believing in my dreams. I have witnessed the manifestations of my dreams, shining bright like a diamond, breaking down the barriers I faced day by day. Even though I had suffered in pure darkness, I am now living a joyful life. My amazing dreams coming true made me BELIEVE.

Remember, you are more than a conqueror. Unleash the warrior power inside you by believing in YOU! Let your light shine now. It is your time to brighten the world by shining brighter than any precious stone. Shine so bright you can't help but realize your value. You must realize that you are meant to face different hurtles and challenges head on. If I can do it, you can too.

Are you ready to bring more light to the world? Here is a rocking challenge! Stand up, look in your favorite mirror, smile and hold your chin up, and speak with authority:

"I have value. I will let the light of prayer, peace, passion, purpose, principles, prosperity, and perseverance shine right through me. I will become victorious and I choose from this day forward to come out of hiding and shine."

ROCK it... Let the challenge begin!

Biography

Nichole Peters is an international motivational speaker, CEO, and founder of Women of Love, Power, and Respect, Women Warriors Who Makes It ROCK and Believe in Your Dreams Publishing. Nichole is the producer of The Motivational Lounge, an upcoming radio show powered by Voice America, and the bestselling author of *A Woman of Love, Power, & Respect*. She believes in nurturing beautiful souls. She is determined to teach downtrodden women and youth the power of self-love. Nichole facilitates workshops and social media coaching for organizations, conferences, and churches, which encourages people to claim their blessings and live up to their greatness within. In the last decade, Nichole has witnessed MANIFESTATION like never before.

The youngest of nine children, Nichole was born and raised in a small town called Bogalusa, LA (63 miles north of New Orleans). Nichole has experienced many hardships in life, but has never lost hope that she would one day serve a greater purpose. As a result, God has not only blessed her with four amazing, beautiful children, but He brought her the love of her life in 2005 and revealed to her the potential to be a writer.

Nichole remains a five-star author on Amazon and Barnes and Nobles. Nichole is also a wellness and beauty advocate. She is a diehard advocate for domestic violence survivors. Nichole reaches out to different safe houses for abused women and delivers a message to let every woman know they are beautiful, strong, and can live off true love and not abuse.

Nichole has two shows on *Empowered ConnectionsTV*™, powered by Voice-America, but on January 20, 2017, Nichole will launch her own Believe In Your Dreams network channel powered by RHG Media.

"I have always loved God, but as a youth, I never truly embraced his teachings. In 2010, I decided to put HIM first in my Life. I promised God that no matter what storms I came across, no matter what the enemy tried to do, this would be our new beginning and I would NEVER stop giving him praise, no matter what. I will NEVER GIVE UP AGAIN!"

Learn More...

www.believeinyourdreamspublishing.com

www.facebook.com/luvpowerrespect

www.believeinyourdreamsauthors.com

believeinyourdreamsproductions@gmail.com

On the Brink of Brilliance
Kathleen Zemansky

My life seemed nearly perfect, almost a fairytale. I was in love and jet-setting around the world in private airplanes, yachts, and luxury cars with a home base in Italy. I believed with all of my heart that our fifteen-year relationship would last forever. Life threw me a curveball at the age of 42 when suddenly and abruptly the relationship ended. Starting over wasn't part of my life's game plan. I was in shock and devastated over it all. I was emotionally wiped out, but I wasn't brain dead. There was something inside me that yearned for a better way to live out my life moving forward.

I had read a bit about Feng Shui, the art and science of placing objects like desks and beds, or even new buildings constructed to harness the positive energies of your environment to improve your living conditions and empower yourself and those around you. This sounded like the tool I needed to get back into the game of life, so I hired a Feng Shui consultant. Within days, I experienced the positive impact of strategically placing objects and creating a different flow in my life. It was like having superpowers. I had two choices: be unstoppable, or be a victim of circumstance. I chose to be Superwoman. It was in that moment I knew that once I got through the heartbreak, I would help others. My calling had found me.

Becoming a Feng Shui consultant was not as easy as I had expected. When I first entered the Feng Shui arena in the late 90's, the industry was quite shrouded with secrecy encrypted from the East with all its potential. Conversely, the western version made outlandish promises all the way to kooky. In addition, Feng Shui is typically a patriarchal system, which didn't allow space, or give much credence to, a western female Feng Shui practitioner.

When I started studying Feng Shui, it was really more from a personal perspective and I constantly spoke about it to friends. They started asking my advice on how to set up their home or offices. It was a lot of fun, but I also honored the methodology and my limitations. I decided that if I was going to give life-changing, transformational advice, I needed to get the proper cultivation. Fresh out of my initial trainings, I would readily offer my services to people and they would take it, especially since I was giving away *free advice,* yet I was paying hundreds and then thousands of dollars for my trainings. I wasn't charging for my valuable time, expertise, or worth. Little did I know this was my first sign of hiding.

The deeper I delved into my studies and my practice as a Feng Shui consultant, the more resistance I encountered. To many family members, friends, and businesses, my career choice seemed too esoteric. I was told, "You are so intelligent and creative. Why don't you become an architect with your savvy sense of design?" Looking back, it might have been the easier road, but working with the subtle energies of the universe was too enticing for me to walk away from. I continued on my exploration to the true meaning and powers of Feng Shui.

When Feng Shui arrived in the U.S. in the early 60's, some things got lost in translation. This intricate system, to understand and practice, requires the time and expense that it does to receive a doctorate. Unfortunately here in the West, Feng Shui got belittled into an add-on service for interior designers and professional organizers. This is one of the reasons Feng Shui lost some of its credibility in the western world.

In addition, there were loads of weekend workshops with people coming out of them as self-proclaimed Feng Shui "masters" in a mere three days! There were floods of books in the marketplace that were really harming the true essence of Feng Shui, promoting and selling gimmicks and trinkets, with claims that if you placed leaded crystals or other inanimate objects like a photo of a couple in a certain area or painted a wall a specific color, you would find a fabulous life partner or make loads of money. All this further tarnished the validity of the industry. I knew from a logical and soul level that the Feng Shui system that conquered and ruled empires in ancient China wasn't done by placing crystals in a certain corner of a building.

Honestly, the Feng Shui being presented in the West didn't make me proud to be in the industry, which tended to make me cover up what I was doing, but it also became my mission to bring credibility and proper awareness to the truth about what I was doing. At the time, I didn't know the vehicle to deliver my message but I was determined to change the face of Feng Shui in the West from a fad to a strategy that every business owner would incorporate into his or her business model for success.

I'd become guarded about discussing my Feng Shui practice and how much I was investing in my research. I continued to study and it became clear that I was attempting to break a glass ceiling in the predominately male-centric Asian industry where Feng Shui is rooted. Feng Shui is like a computer's operating system encrypted with formulas and pathways based on thousands of years of empirical data. In Asia, women are just not considered smart enough to tackle such a topic. To date, rarely does one hear about a famous female Feng Shui master, let alone one held in high esteem.

There were a few other hurdles that started to appear in my own personal relationships as well. When I began my practice, I was single. I found that some of my dates were embarrassed by what I was doing and they requested that I not mention Feng Shui to their friends and family. I couldn't take part in that masquerade very long before moving on. Since Feng Shui is not regulated, there tends to be a great many novices and charlatans in the industry. I've had several concerned people try to convince me I shouldn't be doing Feng Shui, and if I really wanted to pursue this path, then "at least call it something else!"

In my own industry there are stigmas. In 2005, I interviewed several Feng Shui Masters from different schools of thought to obtain a deeper understanding of this industry in the western world. I always show up for my appointments impeccably groomed and in professional business attire. One of the male masters I spoke to said, "You don't look like the typical female Feng Shui consultant."

In dismay, I asked, "What does a female Feng Shui consultant look like?"

He responded, that in his experience, they looked like dumpy, middle-aged housewives, with flowing tie-dyed tent-like dresses, long disheveled hair, no makeup, and Birkenstocks.

As I proudly stood my ground, waving my hands across my body, demonstrating my appearance, I replied, "This is the new norm." It was disappointing to learn that other female consultants had left that impression. I was delighted to be the one breaking the mold.

Unfortunately, stereotypes abound. Over the years, I have attended galas, fundraisers, and other high-end events where I was either told to my face or I overheard people whisper as I walked away, "She sure doesn't look like a Feng Shui consultant."

In many senses, it's easy to hide when you are a pioneer in a country where the people have never heard of Feng Shui, don't know what the term means, don't believe in it, are afraid of its power, or think it's a hippie-dippy thing to do.

I *was* hiding though, and the way I self-sabotaged myself the most was to stay extremely busy and do very well at not making any money at all. I was attempting to do my own bookkeeping, housekeeping, and *countless* hours of administrative work. I was my own worst enemy. I worked over 60 hours a week, seven days a week, working *in* my business instead of working *on* my business. My numbers clearly revealed that I could not afford to hire an admin on which I could offload this work, so I continued to hide behind the excuse that I didn't have the money to make changes.

I was fortunate enough to find love again and marry, but there came a tipping point in my life and business where I was constantly stressed, sleep deprived, and arguing with my husband. This mismanagement of my time and wisdom was costing me a lot. I had a serious conversation with myself about whether or not I wanted to continue on this same path or break free and find team members with the skills to help build my business.

This is when I realized I could not afford to continue WITHOUT a team. My team makes me look awesome – from my admin to a good copywriter, graphic designer, and webmaster. I also gained guidance from incredible mentors and coaches who encouraged me to think bigger and wider. Thankfully I listened. When I let go of having to do it all myself, I stepped into shining, and this has let me provide gifts and tools to support others to truly shine in their life and business.

Collectively my team helped me create my business astrology software, www.FREEBUSINESSASTROLOGY.com, and my TimeBlazr™ Business Management System technology, based on the ancient wisdom of the Chinese Calendar with up-to-date modern applications http://www.5elementsgroup.com/business-timing/

The biggest way I have come out to shine is through my weekly radio program on the VoiceAmerica™ Business Channel, www.IlluminatingFengShui.com. I am honored and excited to be on a mainstream business channel, not a new age or alternative channel. My mission is to serve, through all my products and services, by delivering the highest level of Business Feng Shui Mastery™, Business Astrology, and favorable timing through the TimeBlazr™ to an international audience. I help empower others with the wisdom utilized for millennium by governments, corporations, and affluent people in the East, and it now guides my life.

If I had the option to start over, what might I do differently, and what advice I would offer others?

1. Charge for your services and expertise immediately, relative to the knowledge you acquire. Train to be an expert in your field and let your clients know that as you grow, you can serve them on a higher platform. That means a rate increase concurrent with your upgraded skills and wisdom. Charge your worth always, and don't compromise.

2. Believe in what you do on a cellular level. If people attempt to talk you out of your passion, ask yourself how committed you are to bringing your wisdom to the world. Know that you are on the brink of brilliance and be unstoppable!

3. Within the first twelve months of business, create a digital doc listing every task you do. Put a time and tag on it. Compile the list and mark tasks no one other than you can do. Figure out what other tasks you can work on as a team, and finally what you can delegate 100%. In your digital doc, tag the categories (e.g. your initials, if you are absolutely the only person who can carry out that specific task. "T" is teamwork, and "D" means delegate.) Training good people is key and knowing how much time a task is going to take is essential.

4. Be careful what you say yes to. Your time is precious and something you can never buy back. Always check in with yourself and ask, "Is what I am doing right now moving me closer or further away from my brilliance?"

5. Get visibility as quickly as possible. Seek out speaking engagements, attend networking events, and get on social media. Step forward into your greatness and shine!

Biography

Kathleen Zemansky is a Business Feng Shui Master who is dedicated to helping conscious businesses and individuals harness the power of the ancient wisdom of Classical Feng Shui and Chinese Metaphysics to optimize their success in business and life.

She specializes in Business Feng Shui, Astrology, and Good Timing, and uses these tools to empower her clients to follow their unique birth map, optimize their physical workspace, use their greatest strengths at the right times, and achieve their personal and business goals to craft their destiny.

Kathleen developed her proven date selection technology, The TimeBlazr™ Business Management System, to increase efficiency, productivity, and accountability for her clients, who are both entrepreneurs and professionals. She recently launched her Business Astrology Software, embedded with ancient insight in plain English.

Kathleen is also the host of her weekly radio show *Illuminating Feng Shui* on the VoiceAmerica™ Business Channel, which brings awareness and credibility to Classical Feng Shui and Chinese Metaphysics - a time-proven tool that has been successful for the past millennium. Kathleen interviews business professionals who offer their insights, as well as, weaving in her own perspectives about Feng Shui, astrology, and timing.

Kathleen has several advanced degrees in Classical Feng Shui and Chinese Metaphysics from top-level teachers around the world. She has studied and taught in the United States, Malaysia, China, Tibet, India, and England.

Kathleen's deeper passion is generating greater peace and understanding in the world through cross-cultural communication. She believes her work is a way to pay forward the generosity and joy she has experienced in her world travels and studies. She is thrilled to offer this timeless wisdom for modern usage to help make our world a better place to live, work, and thrive.

Learn More...

Kathleen@5ElementsGroup.com

www.5elementsgroup.com

www.facebook.com/kathleenzemansky

www.linkedin.com/in/kathleenzemansky

Demolish Exhaustion and Overwhelm with the Endless Energy of Joy
Dr. Julianne Blake

Have you ever wanted something really big? It was more than you ever dreamed possible. Then you thought, "Oh no, that could never happen to me!"

Then came the moment when you said to yourself, "Well, what if it could?" You wondered how it would happen, and if you were even worthy. Do you deserve it? Does God love you enough for that? Have you done the right things? Did you care for others more than yourself? What makes you worthy enough to receive those dream gifts? Who decides that anyway, and where did they get the power?

I really wanted to know that when I was just a little girl, maybe six years old. I was lonely and I didn't think I really mattered to anyone – except my dad. But he was gone almost all the time, to other countries on business.

This time it had been six months since he left, and I didn't think he was ever coming back. I knew he wasn't. I was alone. Well, my mom was there, but she was pregnant and depressed, and always busy with the other kids.

Do you ever feel like you are alone in the world and nobody really notices or cares? Maybe you don't really want them to, so you don't tell anyone you need anything.

It's easy to be a hermit. You can train yourself to do that when you're a shy, lonely child.

I wanted so much to find a better way, because I had a dream. It was a big dream! I wanted to be truly happy. I wanted to know that I mattered, that I belonged, and that I was deeply loved.

At our core, everybody wants that. But not everybody believes it's possible, or that they can have it. They haven't experienced it, so they may not even be aware that they want it - yet. But it's a deep yearning inside all human beings, our deepest need in life.

I think it's possible for all of us to have it. Perhaps it takes going inside to know that we can. There is something that happens when we get totally present – whether with another person or with ourselves! We know we belong. We realize we are connected, deeply related. We know: you are my miracle and I am yours. We feel loved and supported. We know that our lives matter.

That's when life feels effortless and we have endless energy. We can do everything we need to do and we are fulfilled, not exhausted and drained. It feels easy to create great products and projects, so we can earn a good living. We are doing what we love, and we feel our joy again. We do deserve that!

I've had a dream since I was young. To me, it felt huge. It was to know and live my purpose and live it in every moment, expressing my full joy, so my overflow is enough to let everyone around me see, feel, and experience it, too! I wanted to do all that while running a successful business that benefits the world.

But things got in the way of me living my dream. I was diagnosed with MS (multiple sclerosis). I was told it was INCURABLE! I had fear, major depression, and overwhelming stress. It impacted my business.

I was sent to an MS support group. Everyone was depressed and had given up. They were complaining about their symptoms and sharing the side effects of their drugs. I went running out of the room (well, sort of!), because it made me feel like I wanted to throw up. If that was support, I didn't want any!

Who could really help me? Everyone said, "No, there's nothing you can do!"

That was NOT true! I learned that when I had a bad fall and suffered a brain injury, which could have killed me. I found the way to bring myself out of serious depression, and even paraplegia! I taught myself to walk again.

At my lowest point, I thought my business was failing. I just couldn't do it all. I struggled, but I got so tired and discouraged. Then, when I thought I was ready to give up and quit, an inner voice came to me. It spoke of my value, my gifts to inspire people who are challenged, with my attitude, my spirit, my tenacity, and my joy.

Things began to shift. I found simple ways to increase my energy and reduce my feelings of overwhelm. I actually stopped over-committing!. That was huge!

Everything turned around. I started to believe it was possible; my big dream could come true! My business took off, my health improved in miraculous ways, and I started doing more speaking.

I found my purpose and joy – and more success than I had ever imagined. I began to share the secrets that worked for me with clients, and they too saw remarkable results in focus, productivity and sales - and how much they valued themselves and their work.

I'm going to share two of those secrets for success with you now.

The first secret is to know your purpose, or your big "WHY?" What is your mission?

When you're connected to your "WHY?" - or your passion - you are coming from an emotionally powerful place in yourself that propels you forward. When you are not, you are doing a "should," a "have to," and you are not acting in joy. That drains and exhausts you. It keeps you from feeling "Endless Energy" and having the impact you want to have. Rather than tiring you, doing what you LOVE excites and feeds you. Doing what you feel passionate about gives you life force and energy. It fuels you to keep going when things get tough! So it's fulfilling your deeper purpose, and it gives meaning to your life. You know you matter. It's not drudgery. You're loving it!

I now help women struggling with anxiety, work stress, or overwhelming pressure to stay vibrant and energized - to be happy and joyful. I show them how to turn that same chronic, draining stress into vital life force, which they can **now** use to stay energized all day long.

When I connected to my own passion, my feelings of overwhelm ended, and my exhaustion melted. I LOVE my work. It reflects my purpose. It fills me up.

So tell me, what do you think your purpose is? If you're not really sure, try asking yourself this question: What do you LOVE to do? What do you do for no particular reward, easily, just for fun? Maybe you don't even feel you have to get paid. Uh, Oh! (A wink and a chuckle!) Now that's a no-no! **That is your gift!** It's what you are naturally good at. That is what you should do and get paid well for, so you can make great income, with a lot of ease and no stress.

Now write down your BIG WHY statement. Why do you do THAT? Put it on the wall in your office, your kitchen, your bathroom, and any place you will see it often. Read it when you want to give up, or you feel stuck, as a reminder. That's your purpose!

We discover your purpose and your passion in sessions with me and in all of my programs! This is **what most empowers you**. Please take any opportunity to use these ideas, and do it on your own, too. Post your BIG WHY purpose statement anywhere you can frequently see and remember it. Be unstoppable, too. It's so much fun!

The second secret is that **the more fun you have, the more money you'll make!** Thinking you can't have fun while you generate income is a big mistake.

Working straight through the day, being glued to your computer, scheduling back-to-back appointments, not eating nourishing food or getting quality sleep, are all careless, seriously draining and debilitating practices. They give you no self-caring moments. There's no nourishment or refueling for you. This makes you feel stressed and overwhelmed. It leads to frazzled nerves, exhaustion, wiped-out immune systems, very low energy, less productivity, crankiness, and irritability.

Stop making this mistake. Learn to have more fun while you skyrocket your income. Enjoy success with no stress and learn to have endless energy now! You'll enjoy energy that lasts throughout the day. You'll have clarity, feel refreshed, be more focused, and be happier. It's fun, rewarding, and nurturing.

A corporate star who was zapped and didn't take breaks because she was afraid she wouldn't get enough done or live up to her high standards, finally went for her much-delayed wellness check-up. Her blood pressure was so extremely high that she was sent to the hospital by ambulance immediately to prevent a heart attack. Now she is getting coaching! She has started taking breaks. She is rewarding herself with fun things that give her pleasure. She's happier, more productive, makes more money, and has more time for play with loved ones.

You can avoid this. Do what you know matters. Schedule time for you. Reward yourself. Get a delicious drink. Set the alarm on your cell so you can get up and walk - away from your desk. Move your body. Go outside. Dance. (You can learn to dance. After all, if I can dance, anyone can!)

Another way to cultivate endless energy is to have a brief, guided meditation. Close your eyes and imagine this:

You breathe deeply, taking in fresh, vital energy. Again, take a deep breath, and as it goes out, release all negativity and toxic energy from your body. Another gentle breath in, and feel your body start to let go and relax.

Now, a beautiful angelic being - or fairy godmother - or spiritual presence (someone who loves and appreciates you unconditionally) comes close to your shoulder and whispers in your ear. What they are saying is the most loving and supportive thing anyone has ever said to you. They profoundly appreciate your great gifts and encourage you to share them in your life and your work. You feel so special. You know you are immensely loved. Your life matters. You are expanding into your most magnificent self, right in this moment, and you know this Being, this Presence, is your special being that will come before you any time you call it. Sure of this, you happily bid it farewell for now, and receive its blessing, bringing that Love into your life. It is yours, and you are so cherished.

Now you come back to the room, feeling full and overflowing with a loving presence to share. Open your eyes to your new world. You can remember or re-read this experience whenever you wish, or whenever you dream, or when you take action to expand in a new direction.

Will you do this? Please write or email or chat me, and let me know how it works for you. And what you'd like more of. I would love to hear from you. You'll enjoy participating in this - and seeing results in your life. Greatest blessings to you, always!

Each one of us is deeply loved and we matter immensely, because we are unique expressions of the Divine Essence. There will never be another you, and you are the only one who can share the magnificence of who YOU are and your beautiful Gifts with the world.

Biography

Julianne Blake, PhD is a leading authority on using Stress Transformation as a powerful, primary path to wellness and personal power. She helps over-worked, over stressed and overwhelmed business owners double their Energy and double their Profit! She has been inspiring - and empowering - women through her speaking, writing (*The Success Secret,* bestseller co-authored with Jack Canfield), coaching, and private therapy practice for over thirty years. She is often called "The Joy Doctor."

Dr. Blake lives her great passion for doubling, tripling or even 10X-ing (yes, magnifying times 10!) your personal power through compassionately caring for You in Mind, Body and Spirit. With her doctorate in clinical psychology, license in MFT counseling, certification as a Success Coach, and training in Neuroscience, she teaches you to heal the mind/body from within by simply re-training your brain.

Her mission springs from her hunger to overcome the trials of her own degenerative disease (multiple sclerosis) rather than be a victim of it. She dedicates her life to guiding women who face life-threatening cancer, anxiety, and disabling chronic stress to triumph over all physical, emotional, spiritual, and business challenges. By word and example, she leads you to take charge, move through obstacles with grace, and profit greatly, in a life you truly love - with passion, and a heart filled with gratitude!

Learn More...

www.EndlessEnergyNow.com

www.facebook.com/JulianneBlakePhD

http://twitter.com/julianneblake

www.linkedin.com/in/julianneblakephd

Impact the World through your S.M.I.LE.S. and Shine!
Shamaine Peters

Impact of Positive Thinking

Parish and I started receiving treatments for our illnesses. Our family wouldn't let us do much, so we suffered together. At school, students bullied us because Parish and I looked and acted drastically different. We were forced to go to different classes due to our new disabilities, so kids laughed, called us "special", and mocked us. Even sick, we got into fights because we hated the mocking stupidity of our classmates. Parish was much sicker than I was, but you couldn't tell because he confronted the bullies, but eventually, Parish had to stop going to school. His cancer had grown significantly worse and he revolved in and out of chemo treatments.

My mom took me to the children's hospital in New Orleans to see him as often as she could, but I never got used to the experience of seeing so many kids, my age and younger, with failing health from devastating and often terminal illness. Parish and I would go to the game room at the hospital to play until he was tired. It depressed me that the most energetic person I'd ever met could barely stand for an hour without getting fatigued. I'd gaze at him with anxious eyes, but he'd always give me this mocking grin.

"SMILE, cousin. Everything will be alright." I'd frown and protest, but Parish would shake his head. "Stop worrying. I am going to get better. I'll be back soon, wait and see. Meanwhile, you watch your back and don't let anyone bother you at school while I'm not there."

There is power in positivity. After seven months of numerous treatments, Parish did get better, his cancer went into remission, and he returned to school. I was ecstatic about him being home where he belonged. He had to be more careful and I had to ignore occasional flare-ups, but we were back together playing, with huge SMILES on our faces.

Impact of Sickness

I'll never forget that Monday morning Granny woke me for school at Auntie Vanessa's house. I had been a guest at her place for the entire weekend and had spent every moment having a wonderful time with my favorite cousin Parish. Our mothers were sisters who'd had overlapping pregnancies. As a result, Parish and I were knuckled-heads born months apart who'd more than bonded. If one of us felt passionately about something in particular, the other did too. Parish obsessively loved any sport that had to do with a ball and that weekend, I'd spent hours on Saturday and after church Sunday playing kickball, baseball, volleyball, basketball, and even tag football.

By the time Granny came to get me from Auntie V's house, I didn't want to get up because I was in extreme pain. For some inexplicable reason, my body felt like a train had run me down. All my nerves, muscles, and tissues screamed in alarm. My body's joints were so swollen that, as I was getting prepared for school, I could barely force myself to hobble to the bathroom. When I raised the toothbrush, I noticed a rash had spread over my fingers. My hands looked like they'd pop any minute. My ankles were swollen and ached terribly too.

I remember calling my mom on the phone. She worked about an hour away from where my aunt, granny, and most of my family lived. Mom insisted that I stay home. "Do not even think about going to school," she ordered in her no nonsense tone. "I'm getting off soon, and everything will be fine. I'm going to hang up now and call the pediatrician's office to get you seen immediately!" The unusual symptoms terrified both my granny and mother. I'd been born prematurely, and as a result, had been receiving treatments to overcome a few other challenges.

Hours later, at the doctor's office, I'd been given a ridiculous number of tests to figure out why I was suddenly moving around like an eighty-year-old woman. Finally, before releasing me, the doctor talked to my family.

"We think your daughter has early onset arthritis. The genetics run in your family history, but we can't confirm anything until the bloodwork is done. For now, I'd recommend that you limit her activity and not let her play in the hot sun until we get to the bottom of why her body is painfully enflamed."

I remember rolling my eyes at the pediatrician. I was a kid and arthritis was an old person's disease. *How dare he tell me I can't play outside!* I fumed. How could I explain to my cousins, especially Parish, that I couldn't go outside? Swollen joints would not be considered a legitimate excuse, not for one second. I couldn't understand why I had to struggle. I'd already been diagnosed with an Emotional Behavior Disorder (EBD) and I struggled in school. My asthma flared up every time I ran too fast, so I had to take my pump out to inhale before I could go back to playing. I wanted to be like other kids. I cried the entire trip home.

As soon as we pulled up to my granny's house, my oldest cousin, Parish's brother, ran out hollering that something was seriously wrong. My family rushed in and found Parish unresponsive on the floor. He was rushed to the hospital. My granny, who my family all called Ma'Dear, sat shocked in a state of disbelief in the lobby of the hospital until the rest of my family came to stand vigil over Parish. My cousin was then rushed to a specialty hospital in New Orleans because they had found a malignant tumor in his neck. Soon after his transfer, my cousin was diagnosed with neuroblastoma, a form of cancer. One week later, test results came back and I was diagnosed with the auto-immune disease juvenile arthritis. My family was devastated.

Impact of One Phone Call

Towards the end of the school year students had mandatory testing for the state of Louisiana. I scored so badly that red flags were raised. Officials called an IEP meeting with my family where the school psychiatrist and the teachers told my granny and parents that I was falling behind. They brainstormed ways I could become more successful through additional classes, services, and tutoring. But no matter how many suggestions were given or how many options were presented, there wasn't a chance I could conceivably stay on the same level as the other kids my age and pass the fourth grade. I was beyond devastated, mostly because Parish and I wouldn't be in the same grade. I was hurt and sad and I questioned in my head, *Why me?*

My family focused on one goal: to get me to retain information so that the next school year, I could pass. Daddy provided my mom with the funds to find a tutor. Mom worked overtime to fund test preps that would help advance my studies. Things were turning around, and I was doing so much better, until my mom received a phone call that changed my family, and my life, forever. Parish cancer's had come back more aggressively.

Six months later my best friend in the world was GONE!

How One Life Can Impact Your Life

Parish's death ripped me apart, mind, body, and soul. My heart couldn't handle being broken like that ever again. I became withdrawn and experienced panic whenever one of my family members or friends caught a minor cold. Every cough or fever freaked me out, I was terrified that I would lose them too. My emotional disorder worsened. I was both anxious and depressed, a paranoid, nervous wreck.

In 2005, my mom made the decision to move to Dallas, Texas. She needed a fresh start and wanted to take her kids with her. She wanted to transfer us to a better environment and school system, but I was resistant to the idea. I'd been raised by Granny more than my mom or dad and I didn't understand why I couldn't stay in Louisiana. Dad was upset that Mom made the decision to take me away, but Granny agreed that it was time for me to live with Mom since she'd made positive changes in her life. I didn't agree. My mother was super strict and the idea of being in Texas without Ma'Dear or Dad as a refuge to run to was terrifying.

Mom waited until the school year in Louisiana was out for summer before moving. We ended up in a great school district, however, when I was tested for the fifth grade school year, the scores that came back indicted that my IQ was barely above the mental retardation level. I watched furious tears fall from my mother's eyes after she left that meeting. I still remember what she said to me.

"Shamaine, let me tell you one thing. The doctors and teachers may think you're going to fail, but they cannot tell you who you can become in the future. I moved you away so you could start over and get the resources you need to get where you need to be. But now, I need for you to believe in yourself. Let the power of God strengthen your mindset. You will graduate and you will make A's and B's. What others thought like to killed me. I refuse to let the same thing happen to you."

I remembered how positive Parish had been and how his mindset had given him extra time to smile, live, and play again. Parish's death had impacted my life so much that I'd forgotten the joy he'd brought while he lived. He'd told me to never let anyone bully me. I realized that bullies are naysayers who come in all shapes and sizes. To honor his memory, I had to let go of the fear. I learned to SMILE despite the pain, to keep going and stay focused on my goals.

In fifth grade, I was assigned six resource classes. A few years later I took three. By the time I made it to high school, I wasn't taking any resource classes. Not only did I fight hard to get good grades, I also made up for my repeated fourth grade year by graduating in three years instead of four.

After I graduated, I decided to attend tech school and I worked part-time at Walmart as cashier. Soon after, I was promoted to a pharmacy technician. A few years later, after delivering my beautiful baby girl, I wanted to mentor youth. My siblings and I started the SMILE organization, (Sisters Motivated In Literacy - Excellent Students). The organization was built in remembrance of my cousin, the late Parish Peters, whose smile was brighter than any sunshine. I use my story of a girl named Shamaine Peters, who was diagnosed with mental retardation and became successful anyway, to prove that, even if your IQ is lower than most, that doesn't mean that you're destined to be a failure all your life.

Impact The World and Shine

There's so many ways that you can make a major impact on the world and **SHINE!**

1. Always be willing to learn.

2. Be self-confident.

3. Never have a negative mindset.

4. Think of ways you can help others and do it.

5. Have hope.

6. Count in all joy.

7. Do things that makes you happy.

8. Do not be judgmental.

9. Always remember what you put out is how you impact the world

PRAY – God will bring peace and blessings.

For everyone in this world who struggles with academic challenges and bullies, SMILE, grab ahold to life and know that you are more than enough in Father God's eyes. Have the courage and strength to think big, grow wise, and be strong enough to speak for the voiceless! Go out and impact the world and leave footprints of your journey by blessing others.

Biography

Shamaine Peters is one of the three founding sisters of the organization S.M.I.L.E.S Academy (Sisters Motivating In Literacy Excellent Students). She loves to model true confidence by rocking her fashionista diva style in order to help students who have been bullied due to their disabilities. She focuses on helping students with achieving, believing, and rocking an "I can be somebody too" confidence. Her S.M.I.L.E.S Academy program helps at-risk students who struggle in school by providing them with free counseling, tutoring services, self-esteem boosting sessions, after school learning programs, and by offering training services.

Despite being misdiagnosed with mental retardation due to one IQ test, Shamaine didn't let this diagnosis define her life. With the help of her supportive grandmother and her never-give-up mother, who wanted nothing more than to see Shamaine and her siblings succeed, Shamaine graduated high school in three years instead of four with a rocking 3.0 GPA. She is now the COO of Women of Love, Power and Respect and Believe In Your Dreams Publishing. Shamaine's upcoming book, *Your Diagnosis Should Not Stop You; Let It Motivate You Instead*, has a release date set for November, 2016 and her future upcoming TV show *Winning Smiles Across America* will be launching in February 2017. She is fast becoming one of the youngest female motivational speakers to gain media attention.

Shamaine was born and raised in Bogalusa, Louisiana. She is the oldest out of her three siblings and the loving mother of one beautiful duchess. Shamaine believes that with God on her side, there's nothing she cannot achieve. She brings them an inspirational message: "I am a walking testimony that anything is possible for those who do believe in themselves. Now SMILE...there is hope! You can move mountains if you just simply believe in order to achieve."

Learn More...

www.facebook.com/luvpowerrespect

www.twitter.com/smilesbeautyamerica

www.motivateurmind@yahoo.com

The Dark Night That Spawned My Liberation
Nancy Monson

Awakened out of a fitful sleep, I panic. Where am I? The room looks completely unfamiliar. I don't recognize anything, and once again my heart starts pounding. This is not my bedroom. My mind races and my eyes search to make sense of my surroundings. A strip of light from my left comes into focus. I recognize it as the bottom of a door. Slowly, the dim outline of a dresser, a television, and a drapery-covered window come into focus. A hotel room. Yes! I'm in a hotel room, but where? My mind flips through cloudy memories of the last dozen hotel rooms I've slept in recently.

Then my exhausted mind recalls that I went out after work for a "team building party" with my consulting colleagues who are staffed on this client project with me. I knew I would be out late again, so I made arrangements to stay in a hotel near my client's site instead of driving home.

Before I could relax into realizing where I was, it hit me. I had come to know these excruciating 3:00 a.m. episodes, the anxiety, my racing mind, and my pounding heart propelling me into the dark inner hell of a panic attack. At least, that's what I called them. It was always the same. I'd awaken in some hotel room in the middle of the night not knowing where I was, panic, and then be thrust into a downward spiral of abusive self-talk from my ruthless inner critic. "You have no clue what you are doing. You are worthless. You have no right to be working here. They are going to find out that you are a fraud. You should just disappear. The world and everyone would be better off without you around. You're just making everything worse." I sob and sob, my heart feeling like it will break from the emotional pain. I pray to God to make me disappear and stop this inner torment.

Eventually, the voice quiets and I stop crying. I stagger into the bathroom to wash my face and then collapse into bed in the hopes of a couple more hours of sleep before I have to be back at my desk and lead my team.

The truth is that I was enormously successful at my job - so successful that I had been promoted at record speed after being hired by a prestigious consulting firm right out of business school. The project on which I was staffed was a huge success. It had skyrocketed me to the executive level and opened the door to a lucrative and well-respected career. I should have been ecstatic, but I was miserable, exhausted, and in serious danger.

I didn't know it. Not until I cautiously shared my reoccurring panic attacks and feelings of hopelessness to a close friend. Looking back, I owe that friend my life. She took a risk and shared what she had been witnessing in me for the last several months: the slow deterioration of my mental stability. She explained what severe chronic stress, massive hours of work, and consistent sleep deprivation can do to one's brain chemistry. She urged me to get professional help. I was stunned! I was in total denial that I was seriously ill. I thought I just needed a little rest, a week off to recover. Fortunately, I trusted her and made an appointment with my doctor.

As I started sharing with my doctor what I'd been experiencing and my symptoms, I began to sob, asking if he would grant me a week's time off to help me rest. I was shocked when he said, "No!"

What he told me threw me into a state of disbelief. He said I was suffering from anxiety and depression and that I needed three months off! That wasn't possible. I was just tired. I just needed a little rest. I couldn't be "mentally ill!" He insisted I take three months off, wrote me a referral to a therapist, and gave me a prescription for Prozac.

That was the beginning of my road to recovery and more importantly, my spiritual awakening. It was the midlife crisis that changed my life forever. It took me the full three months to be well enough to start back to work, but it wasn't until years later and a completely new life that I truly felt I'd healed the brokenness in my body, mind, and spirit.

I am a recovering overachiever. By the time I crashed from severe burnout, I had already accomplished tons, even though my ruthless inner critic had convinced me that I was a failure. I had shattered sales records in two different jobs, graduated on the President's List with a BS in Mathematics, and tackled mountaineering, rock-climbing, and ice-climbing. I scaled Denali, the highest peak in North America. I had received accolades for masterfully facilitating *The Seven Habits of Highly Successful People*, and I earned my MBA from UC Berkeley, one of the top business schools in the world. But all that did not matter in those desperate moments of self-abuse.

You see, the roots of my overachieving superwoman syndrome stem from a deep desire to be good enough for my mother's praise.

A first generation college graduate, I'm the last of five children of poor "dirt farmers" from the Ozarks who immigrated to California during the Great Depression. I had no support from my mother to have a career after high school. She believed that "good Christian women" get married and raise children.

Neither my father nor my mother finished high school. When they first arrived in California in 1936, they worked the fruit harvest as migrant farm workers until my father landed a steady job with the local utility company, tending the ditches that delivered water to the gold mining communities in the Sierra Foothills. My father was a devoted hard worker, accomplished at his job, but he was passed over for promotion in favor of younger men who had college degrees. He saw firsthand the value of education.

However, my mother had a very different life. She was a homemaker. She never held a job or even learned to drive a car. Her world consisted of her family, her church, and the television shows of the 1950s.

As a young teenager during the cultural revolution of the 1960s, I was deeply influenced by the television shows featuring single, independent women with careers. I didn't want to be a housewife. I envied men who seemed to have all the options. I was really smart. I did well in school, and my career counselor encouraged me to apply to university.

My mother didn't get it. She really felt it was senseless for women to aspire to a career. "God designed women to be mothers and wives," she would tell me. She just didn't see the point of college. She frequently compared me to my two older sisters. They didn't go to college and were, at that time, a secretary and bank teller. Why couldn't I be like them? She forced me to take shorthand and typing in high school when my science teacher wanted me to take advanced physics. It was totally outside her world to even conceive of the possibilities that were opening up for women as a result of the feminist movement.

I wanted her to support me in my dreams and aspirations, but that never occurred to her until very late in her life. And so, up until my crash, I spent much of my life trying my best to win her approval of the very different life I chose. So much of what drove me to be the best—to excel in whatever I did—was my deep longing for her to see me and celebrate me for who I was, not who she wanted me to be.

During my recovery, I worked with a therapist, and a significant aspect of my healing was releasing the huge anger and sadness I carried for not being seen and supported by my mother. I realized that I had internalized and amplified her criticism of me. My ruthless inner critic raked me over the coals to the point that I was left a broken spirit lying in a puddle of my tears. It was a very dark time in my life, but as I've gone on to become a guide for women who are navigating life changes, I have discovered that it's not uncommon for women to doubt their worthiness.

A year and a half after I was diagnosed with anxiety and depression, I discovered Transcendental Meditation. During my recovery, I read many books on spiritual truths that touched me to my core. It awakened my spirit and helped me to realize that the life I had created was not the life that I deeply wanted. Leaning TM transformed my life in a matter of weeks! I left my job, partner, home, and life and moved to Fairfield, Iowa, where I enrolled in a second Master's program, studying ancient Vedic wisdom and technologies of consciousness at Maharishi University of Management. It was a major transformation. It changed the trajectory of my life and spawned the life I live today.

After returning to California, I began to rebuild my life. I attended numerous training sessions and launched my own business as a life and executive coach. Outside of my corporate coaching practice, women were coming to me seeking help navigating their midlife crises, which were similar to my own. All the inner work I did, the trainings I completed, and the wisdom I gained were now coming to fruition to help women who struggled to release their own inner doubts and demons, find meaning, and create lives that truly made their hearts sing and their spirits soar.

What I have learned from my own painful journey and bearing witness to the journeys of the many women I have guided is that we desperately need another "women's liberation." So many of us carry the self-deprecating and self-doubting beliefs that we are not "good enough." We need an inner liberation to be able to fully express our true brilliance and shine as we are intended. We each have a story that we need to transcend to truly embrace our unique gifts, talents, and purposes. This is my calling—to support women through their inner liberation from their own limiting beliefs and self-doubts so they can fully express their gifts.

At the World Peace Conference in 2009, the Dalai Lama said western women will save the world. I truly believe that to accomplish this, we must first save ourselves. The world needs women's wisdom, and I believe it needs it now! We are on the brink, at a profound crossroads in our human evolution. The wisdom of women is needed to help humanity navigate this dangerous time in human history. It requires that we do our inner work of liberation to fully embrace our unique gifts and talents, freeing those gifts to bring about healing and change.

I love my mother, and I am eternally grateful to her for the wisdom I have learned on the path she and I traveled. It's been ten years since she passed on, and I now feel her support and encouragement - something she couldn't give when she was alive. Without the journey she and I traveled together and the wounds I encountered and healed, I wouldn't be the woman I am today—empowered, grateful, at peace, and able to help women transcend their self-limiting beliefs about themselves and find their vital place in the world.

If this story resonates with you and you know there's a greater you yearning to be born, please reach out. Don't be shy; I'd love to hear your story! We are not meant to make the journey alone. Without my dear friend who took the risk to reach out to me, I shudder to think of where I would be today.

Biography

Nancy Monson, MA, MBA, CPCC, possesses a rare combination of skills, talents, knowledge, and experiences that makes her gifted at coaching and guiding people to be soul-directed leaders, helping them align with their purposes, passions, power, and presence to create engaged organizations that achieve inspiring results. She does this by helping leaders achieve both inner alignment with their core values, natural strengths, and clarity, and outer alignment with their vision, communication, and actions, bringing them maximum success in their leadership role.

Nancy has a long history of working both in the corporate and the personal transformation arenas. For over twenty years, Nancy has coached and guided leaders and senior executives. She has helped hundreds of senior leaders, executive teams, and boards be effective leaders using her unique combination of strategic and pragmatic skills. For the past fifteen years, she has been guiding women leaders struggling with challenging career and life transitions as their spiritual mentor, teacher, and healer. She now combines these two unique skill sets to support leaders who are called to make a greater impact in their leadership. Her greatest fulfillment comes from confidently guiding successful women leaders dealing with difficult and challenging life changes to be powerful and authentic soul-directed leaders.

What makes Nancy unique in her work with clients is the rare combination of her many years of successfully coaching top business leaders, extensive training in the technologies of inner change and transformation, and her own lifelong pursuit of personal growth. This kaleidoscope of training and experience means that Nancy is able to support leaders who are truly ready to bring out their full leadership potential and create thriving, aligned organizations.

Nancy holds an MBA in Organizational Behavior from UC Berkeley's Hass School of Business, an MA in the Science of Creative Intelligence from the Maharishi University of Management, and a BS in Mathematics from Cal Poly, San Luis Obispo. She also has completed numerous trainings with special emphasis in Human Design, Evolutionary Leadership, life and relationship coaching, spiritual guidance, Tantric counseling, Deep Emotional Release™ bodywork, and Reiki energy healing. Nancy is also a facilitator of the 7 Habits of Highly Effective People personal empowerment course and a coach of the Women, Power, and Body Esteem transformation program for women.

Nancy is also an adventurer. She treasures the outdoors and spends as much time as she can hiking the hills around her California home. In her years of travel and outdoor adventure, she has hiked the Sierra Nevada, Andes, Himalayas, Alaska Range, Brooks Range, and the Rockies. She has backpacked one range or another during every season of the year, climbed frozen waterfalls, numerous rock faces and mountains, and camped on snowy glaciers. Her greatest accomplishment was climbing Denali, the highest peak in North America at a time when it was uncommon to see women in such sports. She believes nature is immensely healing and transformative, taking us to a deep place of inner connection with our own true nature.

Learn More...

https://www.facebook.com/nlmonson

https://www.linkedin.com/in/nancymonson

https://twitter.com/Nancyne

Section 2: You Are Beautifully and Wonderfully Made!

In this beautiful section you will hear stories of amazing experts that will encourage, inspire and remind you that you are truly beautifully and wonderfully made! Enjoy this transformational set of chapters that will speak into your soul the truth that you are beautifully and wonderfully made for such a time as this. Each author shares their story, truths, and powerful actions you can take to help you believe you are beautiful and wonderful just as you are! We believe in you and can't wait to see you come out of hiding and SHINE!

Warmly,

Rebecca Hall Gruyter, Book Compiler and Empowerment Leader

Unmask Your Beautiful and Authentic Radiance to the World
Ron Coquia

In the early moments of your life, you were radiant. Life was a wonderful gift that you received with deep curiosity. You took in every experience of the world around you with all your senses, engaging every fiber of your being. You expressed yourself through the purest form of joy, love, and wonderment. You were free.

Knowing little of the meaning of fear, you hungered to experience the endless possibilities the world offered you. You naturally allowed yourself to feel every flavor of emotion as it flowed through your vibrant body. Whether it was joy, laughter, excitement, surprise, anticipation, or sorrow, you experienced it fully, and you responded by freely expressing your unique essence out into the world, shining your authentic radiance.

Whether or not you remember that powerful time in your life, that experience holds the seed to stepping out of hiding and learning to feely shine your deepest authentic radiance. You see, you already know how to shine, so let's take a moment to plant that seed and remember. I invite you to close your eyes, take in a deep, relaxing breath as you let go of the tension of the day, and allow your imagination to take you back to a time of innocence and purity. Allow the energy of play and imagination to guide you, even if your memories were too distant to remember.

Imagine, if you will, a time when you were little and when the world seemed so new. Take yourself on an exploration of your early childhood memories that hold the feelings of joy, wonder, and freedom. It could be when you first played in the park, rode on a tricycle, or danced to the rhythm of music. Allow yourself to feel every sensation that your body experienced. What did you see? What did you hear? What did you feel? Did you notice a sense of joy, wonder, and aliveness inside of you? Hold that sensation in your heart as a seed of inspiration to live with that same authentic radiance of aliveness again.

So, why don't we experience the world with the same authentic joy and freedom we had as a child? It's because we all had childhood experiences where we felt unsafe freely expressing our joy. It may have come from a time when we felt judged, shamed, humiliated, betrayed, rejected, threatened, or hurt. Whatever the experience was, we may have unknowingly allowed it to define us, poisoning our joyful self-image and replacing it with fear. Every time we felt this fear without resolve, the fear got stronger and stronger and stronger until it reached a point where it became more important than our freedom to express our joy, our spirit, and our passion. The more you spent in this space of fear, the less you expressed your truth and the more you gave your power away to those that you felt had hurt you.

But you're resilient, and you eventually learned to protect yourself from this fear by hiding behind a mask that showed the world what you thought they wanted to see while shielding you from the pain. The deeper the fear or trauma, the more elaborate and convincing these masks became. In fact, the masks may even start to feel good when you put them on because they made you feel strong, intelligent, successful, popular, beautiful, perfect, or invisible. Like the mask of a superhero, sometimes you wore it with pride. But what are you really experiencing, feeling, and believing underneath your mask? Are you really shining your true and authentic light?

I know about masks because I lived behind one much of my life. I once wore the mask of "success." In my 30's, I found myself working at the heart of Silicon Valley for the tenth largest city in the United States.

I was earning a six-figure salary managing information technology for five departments. I got six weeks of vacation per year and had a generous pension plan that would allow me to retire at the age of 55. I lived in a million dollar home in a beautiful suburb in the San Francisco Bay Area with my wife and our amazing son. We were debt free, had everything we wanted, and on top of that, I loved everyone in my life, including my in-laws. I worked hard to build that life. I read many books on personal growth and development throughout the years, so I could continue to build upon my "success." I felt like I was creating the perfect life for me. But all of that was about to change.

One day I was on my way to Disneyland with my wife and my very excited four-year-old son. As I stepped off of the shuttle bus to the park, I got a phone call from my cousin Rhoscoe. I joyfully answered my phone, "Hi, Rhoscoe, we just arrived at the happiest place on earth. What's going on?"

After an unusual moment of silence, he said "Ron, something tragic just happened. Our cousin, Niño, was just hit by a drunk driver. His injuries were so severe that within thirty minutes he passed away."

I stopped like I had hit a wall of sorrow that washed away almost every bit of joy in my spirit. "What?" I couldn't believe it. Niño was only twenty-one years old. He had his whole life ahead of him.

That event in December of 2010 struck me to the core. What amplified that experience even more was that the upcoming year was to be my 40th birthday, and during milestone birthdays, I find myself in deep contemplation, questioning my life's meaning and direction.

After I overcame the initial shock of losing my cousin, I noticed a thought forming in my mind. *That could have been me* ran through my thoughts like a haunting whisper. "I drive over two hours a day to and from work, and I could get in a car crash that could end my life." That horrid thought led to more questions that would forever change my life. "What if I was severely injured in a crash and only had thirty minutes to live? What would I think of my life? Would I be satisfied with the life I lived, or would I be filled with regrets?"

All of a sudden, my whole being was filled with a disturbing mix of sadness and regret. From deep within my soul emerged a feeling of overwhelming emptiness, which was the truth of what I felt about my life. It became clear to me that amid all of my "success," I wasn't really living my life's purpose. I was waiting to retire at fifty-five before I felt safe and secure enough to pursue my true passion. What if I never reached my fifty-fifth birthday? My heart sank.

As I explored deeper, what I found was that my fear of abandonment and rejection was feeding the mask of success that I worked very hard to create. I loved it when people would tell me that they thought I had a perfect relationship with my wife, or how they predicted that I would eventually rise to be the CIO of the organization. That feeling of perceived success made me feel worthy, accepted, and liked, but underneath that mask was a different person.

What I uncovered underneath my mask of success was a scared four-year old boy who had lost the family he knew, all his friends, his toys, his country, and even his language. He had lost his whole world when he was uprooted from his homeland to be reunited with his family who had, years before him, immigrated to the United States without him. Although they were of his flesh and blood, they were strangers, and as much as he learned to love them, his heart longed for the loving family that he had lost: his aunt, his grandfather, and his grandmother.

I was that scared little boy who dearly missed his family, his home, his friends, his toys, and his country. From that traumatic moment in my childhood, I was haunted by the thought that I could be abandoned at any time in my life. The way I unconsciously protected myself was to build a life where everyone liked me and where I had the success and security that protected me. I chose a career not because it was my core passion, but because everyone thought I was good at it. The job I eventually chose was one of the most secure, well-paying, jobs in the world. Don't get me wrong, I did like working in technology as a leader, but it wasn't my true passion. My chosen career was a compromise driven by the fear that lined the inside of my mask of success.

Growing up in the 80s, I was inspired by the likes of Wayne Dyer and Tony Robbins. I wanted to be like them and make a positive difference in the world as a motivational speaker and innovator of personal growth. I wanted to help people to transform their lives to find true freedom, success, happiness, and love. I wanted to invent a revolutionary process of transformation. I even started to outline a transformational process in 2004 during my three hour long train rides to and from work. I called it "Life by Design," but what I was blinded to at the time was that my success was just an illusion for the world to see and not a deeply-rooted success that I felt at my core.

As I contemplated the direction of my life after the death of my cousin, my train of thought led to the emergence of an even more powerful set of questions. "What life do I truly want to live that allows me to express my core passion? How can I start to build a life where I can experience true joy and inner success that resonated to the depths of my soul?"

These powerful questions drove me and spawned a journey of exploration to find how I can live a life of true inner fulfillment. What I realized was that I really wanted to feel the freedom, joy, and wonder that I had felt as a child, before I experienced the traumatic loss that led me to building the mask that I thought protected me from my fears. In actuality, this mask did not really protect me, because deep down inside, it amplified my fears and pulled me away from truly feeling my soul-deep passion and joy.

After a couple of years of exploration, planning, and preparation, I purposely left my job to live my passion and create the life that my soul was calling for. This journey opened many roads and possibilities as I continually discovered and integrated all parts of me that hide behind my mask. I continue to face my fears and learn how to shine my true light into the world. I integrated my passion for art, photography, videography, and technology with my deep passion to serve the world as a transformational coach, and I created a unique business called Transformational Productions that uses video as a powerful vehicle for transformation.

Not only do I help messengers create transformational videos to share their powerful message, but I also use video as a transformational catalyst for those who truly want to free their inner light. Video provides a powerful reflection that can help you uncover the fears that shape your mask. This awareness can help you to dissolve the masks and fears that poison your self-image. For without your masks, you naturally and effortlessly reveal your true beauty and authentic radiance to the world.

If you want to learn more about how you can dissolve your mask to unleash your authentic radiance, I invite you to contact me. I truly want you to shine out into the world with the power and magnificence of a star.

Biography

Ron Coquia is on a lifelong mission to create a powerful transformation in the world. He is a heart-centered visionary who has combined his experience and passion for personal growth, transformation, technology, and the arts to serve the world as a transformational coach, messenger, and producer.

Ron has been an explorer of personal development since 1988, and over the last twelve years, he created a unique and powerful framework for transformation called the 6 Transformational Pathways. Ron used this process to connect to his core essence, embrace his inner power, and overcome obstacles to his own success. In his early 40's, Ron purposely left a successful sixteen-year career as a leader in Information Technology in the heart of Silicon Valley to serve the world as a transformational coach.

As Ron deepened his journey of self-discovery, he embraced the engineer, technologist, artist, and photographer that he left behind when he became a transformational coach. The convergence of all of his passions, skills, and talents led him to a powerful new path to bring more transformation in the world through the powerful medium of video. Ron founded Transformational Productions and launched Transformational Messenger TV to support coaches, speakers, and conscious entrepreneurs with embracing their truth, empowering their message, and expanding the transformational impact they are creating in the world.

Ron believes that it is not what you achieve, but how you hold the light within you that can bring more joy, love, and freedom in your life. It is your beautiful and authentic light that holds the power for your unique transformational message and gifts that the world is hungry for.

Learn More...

ron@transformationalproductions.com

www.TransformationalProductions.com

www.TransformationalMessenger.tv

www.facebook.com/ron.coquia

Sleeping Beauty Awakens
Sumaya O'Grady

Once upon a time, there was a beautiful young woman who was enclosed in a glass casket. She was surrounded by flowers and mourners. She was under a spell and none knew how to awaken her.

That young woman was me. I dreamed about her glass casket at night, again and again. You see, for many years, a big part of me was asleep. How did this happen, and what broke the spell?

The trouble started when I went to a parochial school from kindergarten through ninth grade. It was taught by nuns in a semi-cloistered order who were totally unprepared to teach children. They used public shaming to control the kids. I was shy and I knew I wouldn't survive being shamed. I was terrified to come to school with my homework unfinished, so I stayed awake into the wee hours, night after night, with a flashlight under the blankets, to finish it.

Essentially, my vulnerable self went deep underground and stayed there. For a long time, I felt like the frightened child under the blankets with only a flashlight to guide me. Later, I realized there were other forces at work which also made me want to hide - even from myself.

Looking back, I realized there were two Sumaya's. . .

My soul held the vision of my light-filled life for my younger self until she began to wake up from her deep sleep. My awakening to my true self took courage. Although my journey was long, unique companions and wise advisors arrived in my life when they were most needed.

In my younger years, I had an unreasonable fear of exposure and being visible. If I came out of hiding, I believed I would be found out and killed. These beliefs were barely conscious, and yet they governed so much of my life. I once had a nightmare in which I suddenly materialized inside an old-style glass phone booth on a sidewalk. A car drove by and a faceless person with a machine gun shot me full of holes. This nightmare confirmed my fears.

Another piece of my personal puzzle dropped in around 1990 when I saw the "Burning Times," a documentary about the era of witch burnings that took place in Europe during the 15th to 17th centuries. According to some historians, millions of women were burned at the stake or died in prison of torture. This female holocaust lives on in the collective unconscious of women today and adds to the feeling that it isn't safe to be seen, to be different, or to be powerful.

The film was a revelation that sent shockwaves through my being. I deeply identified with the women who were burned. In my childhood, I had been terrified of fire. It took years to conquer that phobia. I had to leave movies in which a character was burned in a fire. I couldn't watch it. It was just too real.

In the depths of my being, my soul's divine agenda was making itself felt.

I've come to understand that my soul is a deep inner place where my divine spark is enfolded. My soul wants its light to shine forth in the world. It whispered to my unconscious self, "Beloved, step out and shine." My younger self's need to hide simultaneously existed with my soul's need to shine. I was living two parallel lives. Although I was scared, I began to listen to those loving soul whispers.

The first soul whisper that I consciously remember came through when I was in high school. This was a miserable period in my life. We had moved from my childhood home in Indiana to a new town in Florida. I didn't know anyone. My safety net of long-standing friendships was gone.

I did a crazy, brave thing. I signed up for the speech class. I had a strong inner knowing that in my future life, I could not be hampered by my fear of being seen. I knew with certainty that someday, I would be a public speaker. This was scary beyond imagining. However, my speech teacher was so supportive. He was probably my guardian angel in disguise.

In college, every chance I got, I pecked away at my fear, determined not to give into it. In my classes, I gave oral reports instead of written ones. I volunteered to give speeches and to speak on panels. Being visible gradually got easier. In fact, my inner comedian began to emerge in my speeches, which was definitely a sign of life. I was beginning to awaken.

During the college years, my gift for finding heart-friends saved me. It was the early sixties. My new set of women friends were Bohemian, daring, and rebellious. With them, I took big risks and did crazy things like hitchhiking 300 miles from Tampa to Miami to attend a weekend folk festival with little or no money in my pocket and no pre-arranged place to stay. It always worked out. I had many crazy adventures and I realized I loved adventure and risk.

I moved to California with a friend, and our cross-country drive was a rich series of unexpected joys and mishaps. It was the mid-sixties and California was the happening place. I was spreading my wings.

Yet, at the same time, I was still hiding my dreams. Despite my newfound inner freedom and sense of adventure, an old, scared part of myself believed that it wasn't safe to have hopes and dreams for the future. It said, "Don't wish upon a star for your heart's desire. It's dangerous. You'll be disappointed." So I squashed my heart's desires so thoroughly that they disappeared from view for a very long time.

Although I believed that dreams led to disappointment, nothing in my personal life seemed to account for such a devastating belief. After doing years of inner work and healing, I now believe that my fears of disappointment about the future came from my parents and my ancestors. When I learned more about them and their stories, I understood I was carrying their disappointed dreams - not mine. However, it was a long time before I understood this.

Bringing my long buried dreams to light was the scariest thing I ever had to do.

For decades, I followed my passion of deeply exploring spiritual traditions, first as a practitioner, then as a spiritual teacher and healer. Over the last thirty years on this path, I've had to walk my talk. It's impossible to hide if you regularly do spiritual practices and teach others. Long-term meditation practice brings up things from the unconscious realm. Dreams don't like to be buried. They come from the soul, and the soul's light always wants to shine. Dreams create an inner pressure to be set free. If you give them any kind of opening, they will push through your barriers and demand freedom. Mine did.

I began to realize that it was more painful to hide my dreams than face them. One of my spiritual explorations was joining a Tibetan Buddhist meditation center. After a year of being a member, I was asked to give an open house talk at the center. Deep inside, I knew this was important, so I said yes. The talk went well. It felt totally natural, not scary at all. Next, I was asked to teach an eight week class, and each time I taught, my soul was so joyful. Later, I was asked to be a meditation instructor for new people who came to the center and I was assigned students. As I progressed on this path, I knew I had found my place and that spiritual teaching was part of my destiny. Yet I couldn't see how being a spiritual teacher could be a viable career, so I dismissed it as a possibility and didn't give this dream any more airtime.

Ten years later, I joined a new spiritual path and community, and the same thing happened. I was asked to start teaching. Whenever I taught, I felt such a deep sense of rightness and inner alignment, yet I still couldn't see ways to bring this experience more fully into my life.

My soul continued to nudge me. Sometimes a soul-nudge becomes *way* more intense if you don't listen. I became seriously ill during this time and I had to dig deep into my inner resources to survive the illness. Prior to this time, in my day job, I had been doing work I was really good at, but absolutely hated. I would drive to the office building, then sit in the parking lot and cry. I dreaded going inside. I knew something had to change. This was the second major illness in twenty years, and both times the common thread was this: I had been doing work I hated. I was not listening to my soul and was still burying my dreams. I realized I finally had to stop what I was doing, listen within, and take empowered action in the world, no matter how scary. My life depended on it. But I didn't know what to do. I prayed. I meditated.

What happened next was a crazy soul-guided series of events.

I attended a two-day seminar for heart-centered entrepreneurs, taught by a gifted business coach. He led the group through a visualization and interactive exercise that was truly life-altering. In the exercise, I imagined myself on my deathbed in a life in which I had not manifested my true purpose. It was a tragic and frightening scene. Because I had been haunted by that same potential scenario for years, the experience shook me to my core. It was a major wake-up call. I knew I had to take a stand and change the trajectory of my life.

A few years later, I launched my business, Soul-Deep Confidence. Through the programs I've created, my clients experience healings that open the door to their divine essence and inner guidance system. Then, they have the clarity to make decisions with ease and stay aligned with their soul's purpose.

These are the very skills I worked so long and hard to acquire, and now, they are my gifts for the world. The great poet Rumi wrote: "The wound is the place where the light comes in."

I'm now highly visible. I have spoken on many stages and radio shows, and have been interviewed on TV shows. I'm also the co-author of a national bestselling book. I'm being continually guided by my soul. My dreams are alive and well, fueling me forward so that I live my purpose.

Sumaya's Recipe for a Soul-Centered Life

1. Always listen to your soul, and follow your intuitive hunches. At first, your soul's guidance might seem like a very subtle inner prompting. Even if you're not sure where it's leading, follow it. Your soul contains the blueprint for your life. The more you listen, the greater the clarity.

2. Treasure your dreams for your future. Share them with heart-friends. If your dreams seem wildly impractical, don't turn away from them. Unlived dreams become quite painful. Instead, seek out the mentors who can help you bring them into reality.

3. If you're deeply unhappy with the work you're doing, don't let the pain continue. Stop now. Get some mentoring and take inventory of your choices. You don't have to figure this out alone. Keep following Steps 1 and 2.

4. Develop a meditation practice. This clears away the daily concerns long enough for you to see what's brewing underneath. It's challenging in the beginning, and yet it's one of the most worthwhile things you can do hear guidance and get clarity on your direction.

5. Most importantly, cultivate self-love. The lack of self-love is at the bottom of most emotional pain. With self-love, the hard things get easier and you become unstoppable.

Biography

Sumaya O'Grady is a spiritual teacher and healer with over thirty years of experience. She is known as a Soul Alchemist because her transformational healing programs guide her clients into connection with their divine essence and inner guidance.

Sumaya has studied, practiced, and taught many of the world's wisdom traditions, including Tibetan Buddhism, Core Shamanism, and Sufism. She traveled the world and studied at the Dalai Lama's headquarters in India, where she had a profound feeling of coming home. She studied with a Sufi Master from Jerusalem for 16 years, and continues to expand her spiritual horizons.

She is a graduate of the University of Spiritual Healing and Sufism and became recognized as a master teacher and healer in the Sufi tradition. As she walked through all of her of spiritual paths, she was gifted with truly wise, generous, and enlightened teachers. Sumaya has gained an appreciation of the Divine as it manifests in its many forms in people's lives.

Sparked by a health crisis over two decades ago, she began her love affair with the healing arts. Sumaya has a passion for body/mind/spirit healing and combines her spiritual and meditation training with body and breath disciplines. She had a bodywork practice based on Rosen Method and later practiced as a registered Biodynamic Craniosacral Therapist. She also studied a number of other healing traditions, including Yoga, Tai Chi, Chi Gung, Reiki, Process-Oriented Psychology, and many methods of spiritual healing.

Sumaya holds a Master's degree in Counseling Psychology. She was the Administrative Director of the graduate psychology department at JFK University, and was the Director of Continuing Education and Continuing Medical Education at the Institute of Behavioral Healthcare. She was deeply engaged in the UNtraining, a program for helping white people explore the roots of racism, privilege, and unconscious conditioning. She taught diversity awareness workshops at JFK University.

Sumaya feels privileged to witness the transformation that takes place in her clients when they are able to connect with their own inner divine presence and then begin to live from that sacred place.

Learn More...

Sumaya@SoulDeepConfidence.com

www.SoulDeepConfidence.com

www.Facebook.com/ShiningYourLight

Twitter: @sogrady711

Unleash the Good Girl Rebel
Mary E. Knippel

I was the good girl growing up, watching Donna Reed and reading Erma Bombeck. Donna Reed was on TV portraying the perfect 50's housewife, dispensing wisdom and always wearing her pearls. Erma Bombeck wrote funny stories about everyday life and even had a spot on morning television. She was a huge hit, talking about not only making the pot roast, but also burning it!

As a good girl in the 50's, the thought of conflict in any way kept me silent and invisible. I will always be a good girl who wants to be loved, however, today I'm changing my story and coming out of hiding to show up and shine. I refuse to live by anyone's rules but my own any longer. I am speaking up and showing up at the center of my own life, for my sake and for the sake of those I am here to serve with my gifts.

Now, I am the Good Girl Rebel who is rewriting her story and taking charge of her life. A rebel is a person who stands up for her own personal opinions despite what anyone else says. I am no longer passive about frustrating circumstances and disappointing situations. I have learned to give myself permission to live a life unleashed from those parts of the good girl syndrome where I felt compelled to please in order to be loved.

When I was a child, the only rebellion going on was in my head. I was known as shy, quiet Mary. It was expected that I would defer to everyone's expectations and not have a separate opinion or agenda. Compliance meant that I could be included in the group and enjoy the fun, even if it was on the fringe of things - and I so wanted to belong.

The trouble with wanting to belong is that sometimes you get inducted into groups you never would have applied for. Parenthood, for example, seemed like something easily accomplished. But after receiving the puzzling results of "undetermined infertility," I was filling out forms and getting references to prove my worth as a human being. While I was waiting to become a mother through the adoption process, I pursued my other dream of becoming a writer and I enrolled as a thirty-year-old college freshman. The group that really brought out my rebel behavior was when I had the distinction of being the one in eight women who are diagnosed with breast cancer in her lifetime. I was inducted into that group twice!

The groundwork for my rebellion was laid each time I met disappointment and found a silver lining in the dark cloud. "If you don't like something," as Maya Angelou so wisely advises us, "change it. If you can't change it, change your attitude."

During high school, we were assigned to write a research paper on three future career options. Looking out of my small bedroom window on the family farm, I wrote about going to college to study acting. I described becoming a famous actress who could do comedy and drama with ease, was a darling of the London and New York stage, and had conquered the silver screen along with television. I wrote about becoming an accomplished dancer who traveled the world performing for sold out crowds at every venue. I wrote about writing stories that touched the hearts of those who read my words and writing in exotic parts of the world.

Although neatly typed and turned in on time, I received a C+ for the project because my career choices were judged as unrealistic. I was a shy, quiet fifteen-year-old-girl in a small Midwestern community. How could I possibly aspire to be an actress, a dancer, or a writer, for that matter? I had never taken a dance lesson or showed any particular talent for the stage. My writing was confined to my journals and never shared with anyone.

I poured over college course descriptions in secret, and so in the end, I was convinced to take the safe route. My next stop after high school was a one year Secretarial Certificate from the community college. My silver lining there was meeting a nice boy on a blind date. I married him and supported us with my secretarial skills so that he could earn a college degree.

I never gave up my dreams and what I believed my future could hold. I decided that I had enough of making safe choices and waiting for my fantasy life to become a reality. It was time to take action. I wanted something more than advice to *just be patient*, and that popular nugget, *wait and see*.

I quit a ten year secretarial career to pursue my dream of not just a diploma, but a degree from the School of Journalism. During college, my guidance counselor saw me as a flighty housewife and encouraged me to forget about journalism and go back to my secretarial career. I didn't give in. He steered me to the Mass Communication track instead of Journalism because he didn't think I could handle the reporter's curriculum. Little did he know I'd spend the next thirty years as a reporter specializing in personal profiles for magazines, newspapers, and online venues. No, I have never reported from a war zone or sat at a news desk. I have conducted hundreds of interviews with individuals and small business owners and produced stories that reflect who they are and their passion for what they do. I especially delight in supporting women who want to connect with their story...to have compassion for all the parts of their story ...to be inspired by where their story has brought them today.

Proving I could function in the world of academics was powerful for me. The silver lining was spending a quarter studying in London and fulfilling my dream of combining my love of writing and travel. I saw a new me. I spoke up in my classes and had an identity away from my previous life.

After years on the adoption waiting list and just weeks before finishing my final quarter, we got the joyful call that it was time to pick up our baby girl. My life was full as wife, mother, and as a part-time editorial assistant for a weekly newspaper.

Life was wonderful...then that letter arrived.

When the words "breast cancer" are uttered, a suffocating fear and apprehension engulfs you. After battling back twice from that diagnosis, I do not consider myself simply surviving. I am thriving. The second time I received a form letter with the news of an abnormal mammogram (in less than three years) was the day I decided I wouldn't tolerate being treated as a statistic any longer. The first time I was diagnosed with breast cancer, I jumped back to life as usual as quickly as I could. It was safer to continue hiding from that diagnosis and pretend it had never happened. The second time I was diagnosed and received another form letter, I could not hide any longer. I woke up. I paid attention. And that's when I said, "No more life as usual!"

I rebelled against going back to the same old routine and created a New Normal for myself. I learned to make choices in my life to promote my healing process. I decided I wasn't going to be voiceless any longer. I am a vibrant woman who deserves to live a life unleashed. My story has value and your story has value. I am showing up to be seen in the light and to shine my light on those who I am here to serve. I am a mentor, guide, and champion for other women to claim their stories.

I have been free of cancer for over ten years now. My silver lining here is that the gift of breast cancer brought me clarity about what is important in life. You do not need to wait until you have a health crisis to take care of yourself. The time is now to go after your dreams. I practice radical self-care by making me a priority in my own life. I unleash from whatever holds me back from being who I was born to be.

If I could go back and speak to my younger self, this is what I want her to know:

God has bestowed you with superpower. He has written on your heart the mission you are here to perform and given you exactly what you need to accomplish your task. Maya Angelou has said that you must change your attitude if you cannot change a situation. My interpretation of that is instead of "attitude," you insert "story." Change your story and rewrite it where you live your dreams. Despite what the world may tell you, everything you need is within you as you are right now. You are here to make a difference with your gifts of authentic connection, deep compassion, and heartfelt inspiration.

Today, I am coming out of hiding to show up and shine! I have rewritten my story to place me where I can use the knowledge I have acquired from my life experiences to influence and inspire others on this sacred journey we call life. I am on a mission to support reluctant writers to unleash from the stories holding them back as the Writer Unleashed at http://yourwritingmentor.com. My wish for you is that within the story of my personal journey, your own story will unfold in revelations of self-compassion, self-empowerment, and self-discovery.

Wondering how to go about writing your own story...to be the author of your life? It's simple. Grab a notebook and start having regular conversations on paper to get your thoughts, dreams, and longings out of your body! When you show up on the page for as little as five or ten minutes a day, dramatic things will start to happen. Journaling has been my path to discovering my inner wisdom. Both personal and professional goals began as ideas, questions, and considerations within the pages of my journal.

Journaling can be a place for you to start your plans to transform your life. Your story matters and no one else can tell your story from the inside out except you. Don't worry about not knowing what to write. Allow your subconscious to come to the surface and **listen** to what it has to say.

Try an experiment for thirty days and give yourself the opportunity to build your writing muscle in small increments. You can use a notebook, loose leaf paper, index cards, or even the back of junk mail. My suggestion would be to write longhand, as I believe that gives you a stronger connection between your head and your heart. Choose a time of day you will be able to show up on the page consistently, set the timer so you don't watch the clock, and just write. Begin every journal writing experience by grounding yourself first in the present moment by writing the date, time, and a description of your surroundings at the top of the page. You'll be amazed at what treasure you'll discover at the end of your fingertips.

Drop me a note, or give me a call if you'd like to talk about what writing in your journal has stirred up in you.

I am a Good Girl Rebel. I invite you to Unleash the Good Girl Rebel in you. Who's with me?

Biography

Mary E. Knippel, Writer Unleashed at YourWritingMentor.com, transformational author, publisher, and inspirational speaker, intimately understands what it means to be a woman in transition on a journey of self-discovery from the woman you no longer recognize to the woman you want to become. Mary is fiercely committed to support you to unleash your voice, to speak up and shine in your business and in your life as the gift you are to the world, to be the author of your story, and to leverage your impact through writing. Through presentations and programs such as Unleash Your Fame & Fortune blogging course, Unleash Your Authentic Voice, and Living a Life Unleashed, women are able to put their passion and purpose into words. Using the power of storytelling, she helps you gain clarity and confidence to reclaim your voice, rewrite your story, and to unleash your message. You matter; your story matters; and you are the only one who can tell your story from the inside out. You are an extraordinary woman longing to be free to Live a Life Unleashed!

A journal writer since the age of eleven and a journalist for over thirty years, Mary knows the enormous power and healing capabilities of the written word. A two-time breast cancer survivor, she encourages writing and other hands-on creative tools as powerful recovery techniques in her upcoming book, *The Secret Artist*. Throughout the book she chronicles her own breast cancer journey and shares tips about what she has learned to help you move from survive to thrive. She urges every woman to come "home" to herself – to be at home with herself in body, mind, and spirit - and not to wait until she has a health crisis to start making herself a priority by practicing self-love and especially self-care.

Learn more about Mary's classes and workshops, request a complimentary discovery session, sign-up to receive free ongoing writing tips and techniques, or invite her to speak to your group, by visiting her

Learn More...

www.yourwritingmentor.com.

mary@yourwritingmentor.com

http://fb.com/maryeknippel

http://fb.com/maryeknippel.author

Breakdown to Breakthrough
Ronnie Joy Krasner, CSC

YOU DON'T WANT TO KNOW THE TRUTH. As I was driving, I saw those words right in front of me. At that moment, I knew the truth.

A few months prior, shortly after my divorce, I started using the services of a therapist. She was a licensed clinical social worker and clairaudient/clairvoyant intuitive coach. She channeled information from spiritual guides. I was advised by the guides to not date anyone and spend time alone because "you don't want to know the truth."

I didn't want to know the truth? How could that be? I'm the most introspective person I know. The thought of not having a man to lean on, if I followed the guides' advice, was a little scary for me. I married young and the marriage lasted twenty-six years. Once my divorce was final, I started dating again, even though I didn't know what I was doing. I did follow the advice of the spiritual guides and spent time alone walking scenic trails, listening to the rushing sounds of a nearby creek, meditating and praying. And I couldn't stop crying.

A series of coincidences led me to visit Regina, a friend I hadn't seen in a long time. Regina was a therapist. We talked and talked and caught each other up on our lives. She was telling me a story and she said, "...and that's how people who have been sexually abused respond."

I blurted out, "Regina, I think I was sexually abused."

She agreed. She said different snippets of my life came together for her and she thought I fit the pattern. I felt emotionally exhausted and I wasn't ready to explore it. Regina assured me I could wait until I was ready. I took a power nap then left to drive home. On my way, I knew that I had to face this discovery and work it through. And I knew who the abuser was. As I drove, I started doubting myself. Did this really happen to me? And then I saw those words right in front of me, YOU DON'T WANT TO KNOW THE TRUTH. I knew this was the truth...and never doubted it again.

My healing journey began. With therapy and a workbook for survivors of child sexual abuse, I started putting pieces of my life together. My therapist pointed out that the behaviors I had displayed in my past were classic behaviors of sexual abuse survivors. I learned that the abuse had happened to me before I was verbal. I learned that dissociation is a mental process where a person disconnects from their thoughts. That was a common occurrence for me especially when I was engaged in conversation. I thought everyone's thoughts drifted somewhere else. I came to understand why my antenna was constantly up for sex. I was hard wired for it. I learned, on a greater scale, why I was depressed during my childhood and into adulthood. I learned why I had behaved in ways I couldn't understand during my marriage. I began to believe and understand that the emotional, verbal, and sexual abuse I suffered in childhood wasn't my fault.

When I look at the negative effects of abuse in my life, it's hard to imagine that I could have developed strengths at the same time...but I did. That doesn't mean there is a good side to any form of abuse. Recognizing your strengths does not mean you have to minimize your abuse or discount the negative effect it's had on your life. Recognizing your strengths is the way to feel good about yourself despite what's happened to you.

It took time, but I knew the direction I wanted to take in my healing. The process of healing was both painful and liberating. As I looked back on my life, I went from the shy, depressed child to the assured adult whose painful experiences enabled her to have more empathy and compassion. I found my voice. Instead of being quiet and fearful of being criticized for anything I'd say, I trusted that what I said, had opinions about, or cared about, mattered. And if it only mattered to me, that was enough. This was my journey, my time to come out of hiding, time to really believe in myself and know that I was good enough. I had gifts to share and I became a certified life coach.

A large aspect of life coaching is about asking the right questions and, for me, it was a perfect fit. It seemed no one was more curious than me! I made a conscious decision to date in new, healthy ways. That meant putting closure on any love relationship that didn't work out. When the relationship ended, I told that partner, "Thank you for the learning" and wished him luck. I didn't remain friends with a man after the relationship was over. I believed I was sending the Universe a message – I was serious about calling in the perfect partner – and must close the door for the right relationship door to open. I wanted to be in a committed, monogamous relationship and I learned to not have sex too soon.

There were times I was filled with regrets. I'd remind myself, "That's who I was then; that's not who I am now." Gratitude and forgiveness exercises were an ongoing practice and powerfully transformative. Between my life coaching skills and new ways of approaching and responding to men, I developed successful strategies for online dating and dating in the wild. I was attracting better quality men and I had several long-term relationships. I had lived all of my life in Connecticut, but living there was feeling flat. The idea of moving was persistent. I moved from Connecticut to California. I was ready for a new life.

Moving to the San Francisco Bay Area felt like coming home. I met amazing friends and considered them old souls reconnecting. I had challenges, too. They're a part of life. The key is how I'd respond to those challenges. Did I respond from a place of love or a place of fear? I chose love! In California, I established new coaching clients and also continued dating. The same successful dating strategies were working. I met and dated quality men. I was on a mission to meet my mate!

About a year after the move, I was on one of my favorite online dating sites and came across the profile and photos of an intriguing man. He was attractive, witty, and spoke of many things, including his spirituality. And that is what truly spoke to me. Fear of rejection crept into my thoughts. How could I possibly reach out to him? I gave it serious thought and realized, what's the worst that could happen? I finally emailed him. We corresponded. We talked on the phone. We met for lunch. Three years after our first date, we married! Jack is the love of my life and we both know that our relationship couldn't have worked out if we had met each other sooner. I believe in divine timing.

More and more of my coaching clients are single, generally in their 50s and older. A priority for them is to find someone special to share their lives with. They are daunted by the dating scene and unsure how to date after their long-term marriage or relationship ended. Most are frustrated by the lack of results they're getting meeting available, quality men or women. I understood how they felt. I'd been there. I knew the time it takes to feel whole and complete after divorce and the yearning to share your life with that special someone. Dating is different in midlife than it was in your 20s. I teach my clients the successful strategies I created to find and keep a perfect partner. They benefit from my coaching, dating and relationship skills. Over time, they date successfully, have long-term relationships and many get married! I decided to focus my coaching practice on teaching midlife singles how to successfully get back into the dating world. That's how I became "Ronnie Joy, The Midlife Dating Coach."

I know I'm here to make a difference in peoples' lives. I'm here to let you know that there is light at the end of the tunnel. I got in touch with my self-worth and my value as a human being. I grew to love myself and value myself for simply being me. I am here on this planet for a reason. Going through what I did brought me insights that I wouldn't have otherwise had. The truth is revealed when we're able to handle it. Having the memories and knowing it was true, I was able to process the abuse more objectively. Yes, that happened, but it didn't define me. It happened and it gave me more compassion for myself and for others.

You are here for a reason. Be gentle, patient and tolerant with yourself. Let go of anything that impedes you; it's not who you are. Heal the parts that don't allow you to let go and shine.

I invite you to embrace The Four Agreements: A Practical Guide to Personal Wisdom by Don Miguel Ruiz.

1. "Be Impeccable With Your Word." Speak honestly and directly. No blaming, shaming, criticizing, or gossiping. Only make commitments you intend to honor and follow through on.

2. "Don't Make Assumptions." Ask questions and communicate clearly. You are not a mind reader nor can anyone read your mind.

3. "Don't Take Anything Personally." What people say or do has nothing to do with you. It has everything to do with themselves.

4. "Always Do Your Best." Come from a place of integrity and you won't have regrets or self-doubt.

Biography

Ronnie Joy Krasner wants to know... What does transformation mean to you? Dating and relationship expert Ronnie Joy Krasner has seen it defined many ways. Is it a dramatic change or a life-altering event? Going from stuck to clarity? Finding your spirituality? Or, is there a different story?

With more than thirteen years of life coaching and four decades of real life marriage, divorce, dating, and remarriage experience, her view is very different. Unlike many dating coaches, Ronnie Joy, The Midlife Dating Coach, shows you how to up-level and transform your current wardrobe for dating, everyday wear, and professional looks. Inner, authentic beauty manifesting outward is for everyone, every day.

Clients refer to Ronnie Joy as their secret weapon for dating, relationships, and transformative growth. Her coaching skill brings out the best in people. Clients have partnered with Ronnie Joy when they want to successfully find and keep their special someone. She guides clients to create online dating profiles, find potential dates in everyday places, and create a more polished, confident, and authentic look.

Ronnie Joy was living alone, for the first time in her life, after her marriage of twenty-six years ended in divorce. After challenging dating experiences and life coach trainings, Ronnie Joy became clear about her values and self-worth and the man she wanted to share her life with. She developed successful strategies to meet quality men online and in the wild. She took a leap of faith and moved from Connecticut to California in 2005. A year after moving to California, Ronnie Joy met Jack, the love of her life, and they married in 2009.

Ronnie Joy has a B.A. in Psychology. She graduated from The Coaches Training Institute, received Denise Linn's Personal Certification in Soul Coaching®, and is a Silva Method graduate. She developed "Have Them at Hello!", "Dating in the Wild", and "Dump the Frump" workshops and continues to work with heartfelt peers in the dating and personal styling field. Her internet radio talk show, "Right on Time Dating!" features conversations with guests about all things midlife and, in particular, dating. As a speaker, Ronnie Joy's fusion of real life stories and conversational style connects with her audience at an intimate level.

Learn More...

RonnieJoy@TheMidlifeDatingCoach.com

http://www.TheMidlifeDatingCoach.com

http://www.facebook.com/themidlifedatingcoach

https://www.linkedin.com/in/ronniejoykrasner

Stepping Into Your True Authentic Story
Danielle Nistor

I am committed to truth, self-expression, and respect.

Let me share my story with you. It was not until I was about fifty years old that I woke up from a spell and I truly became myself. The story I want to tell here is all about the ways we betray ourselves in life in order to obtain a little bit of approval, love, and a sense of belonging.

But let me get back for a minute to the story. My husband, whom I had been with for twenty years, decided to start a new life behind my back. A part of me was in shock and could not comprehend what was going on. Another part was scared and depressed. Yet the most upsetting thing was that an unknown part of me was loud and extremely angry. This part is the one who finally saved me, helped me wake up and get back to myself as who I truly am. I am grateful to this part of myself that would not tolerate any disrespect from anyone and holds me accountable to be truthful to my needs and to live my life following a code of honor.

Our lives are led by many stories. Some of them belong to us and are told from different angles. Others are a blend of our parents' stories, hopes, and expectations, and still others can be a projection of the society where the person is perceived according to its gender, age, and level of knowledge.

One story about me says I was born out of love as a beautiful baby with big blue eyes. Later in life I worked as a photo model and a runway model, being successful and fully enjoying my work. I graduated International Law, as I wanted to bring more peace, truth, and justice in the world.

When I was thirty years old, a man fell in love with me, proposed to me, and I followed him to America to create my own family. Almost five years later I had a strong spiritual experience in a sacred place, which activated many gifts for me, including the gift of channeling, clairvoyance, and mediumship. I started working as a divine connector, spiritual teacher, and inspirational writer and through God's grace, I saw many miracles happening in people's lives.

Those snapshots of my life sound like a fairy tale, don't they? They are all true, but only if they are seen from one angle of the story.

Another story, the rough one, says I almost died at birth as a premature baby born at seven months, suffocated with the umbilical cord and being thrown into the incubator. I was even declared dead by mistake. A curse or a miracle? My father was hoping for a boy to carry his business further as he did at his turn, and he was disappointed to have a daughter.

I grew up as an awkward kid with very poor social skills due to the fact that my family was not there for me. My father was home only at night due to overwork and my mother was not available to me, mostly because of her depression.

I felt confused and like a misfit in my family and in the world. I was born in the Communist Romania at a time where life was unfolding in a grey shade. My spirit was crippled by the rules and fears and also by a family who was too busy with its own survival. I learned quickly that there was no room for me to breathe as who I truly am neither in that country nor in my own family. My escape mechanism at that time was daydreaming and connecting with my own family - the divine one - a world in which angels, fairies, God, and The Divine Mother were present to wipe my tears and hear my desperation through the eternal question:

am I on the wrong planet? Where and how can I find love between people?

I started school too early as a six-year-old, a nervous child, feeling vulnerable and struggling to adapt into a new environment. We had a new apartment. We had moved into in a new area of the city and the school with a new set of rules and attitudes presented a whole new life.

As a teenager, I wanted to be an actress but I made it as a model instead and later I studied law. Deep down in my soul I felt I was meant to be a healer of some sort and I studied many modalities, being profoundly touched by all of them.

I was oversensitive and I was also carrying my mother's depression, feeling lost in the world of Communism without the freedom of speech or religion.

When I was twenty-four years old I got raped by a friend and I was profoundly traumatized by the shock. I started hiding myself in men's clothes and refraining from wearing makeup in my personal time.

At twenty-five years old, feeling at the end of the rope, I had a strong suicide attempt, which kept me weeks in the hospital. I felt I was wrong, misunderstood, and a problem to others and the only solution I could envision was to remove myself from the world.

Years went by and I married. I moved to the U.S. to discover that I had married a controlling and verbally abusing man. Although my depression was under control, I was unhappy. I asked God to either use me for something bigger than myself or to remove me from this world, as I could not bear the pain anymore.

His answer came soon and it was expressed as a true miracle. During my pilgrimage to Medjugorje, the Divine Mother reappeared to me as she used to do in my childhood. In a vision, she appeared as our amazingly beautiful loving Lady of Peace and told me, "I want you be my peace messenger and bring my messages of love and hope to the world." I stood there crying and spinning in all directions. Her messages were true. I started receiving her messages from that day on and have been blessed with many spiritual gifts and initiations since then.

As I began to regain this close relationship with my divine family, I could see countless miracles in my life and my work. However, I kept feeling ashamed, wrong, and unworthy because my family was not able to accept me as I was and because of my attempted suicide. A part of me would ask repeatedly in my mind, "Why me? How on Earth did she choose me?" I could understand the motherly love and support she gave me as a child to help me survive in a cold world, but I had a hard time accepting her gift and acknowledgement received during my pilgrimage.

My mind would keep tormenting me with sentences like, "Doesn't she know? How can she trust me with her work? Why is she offering me the honor of being her messenger of divine love on earth? Isn't she remembering that years ago I committed the ugliest rebellion, the last sin, refusing the gift of life and attempting suicide? Why me?" It took me many years of inner battles, shame, turmoil, and transformation to get to the understanding that we are innocent and accepted as we are by the Divine and forgave myself.

I started going to personal development seminars and camps, using intense physical experiences to break through my fears, inner doubt, shame, and illusions. Following divine guidance, I was able to discover myself as an empathic. I started healing my inner self.

Today I am grateful to all the hardship in my life that taught me who I am: a child of God, made of faith, and that I am here to stand for truth, compassion, self-expression, and respect.

In a personal message from the Divine Mother, I was told, "You are loved. I did not want you to suffer. It is your soul which chooses those lessons in order to gain compassion and truly understand human suffering through an array of traumatic life experiences so that you can understand human nature and be able to serve humanity through your gifts. I chose you exactly for who you are in order to show people that I am a mother to all of you, especially to vulnerable souls who need my love and support. You are all innocent, lovable, and valuable to me."

The question that I have for you is this: where do you play small in your life? Why? What is it at stake? Are you aware of your why? Is it possible that you gave away your power to someone else?

All is fine. Maybe you wanted to be loved or maybe a part of you felt an urge of being surrounded by peace. Perhaps you just learned a specific role from your parents and assumed it unconsciously, although it was not truly yours to play.

Wake up now! The time has come to become conscious of your life and to take your power back.

It is your life! And only when you allow yourself to be empowered can you be YOU – which is the only authentic role that your soul is here to play.

Being human means always being vulnerable. There is nothing to be ashamed of.

The truth I learned is that even if God himself came to save you, if you are not ready to value yourself, you may not be able to accept the love or the help He offers.

Make peace with yourself. You came here as a shiny spirit of light to spread love, knowledge, and your unique gifts. When you get caught in emotions, traumas, and dramas, please remember who you truly are and quickly take your beautiful Self out of confusion, shame, and guilt. Life experiences are learning experiences meant to empower us and to bring us back to our own truth.

Today I know that the universe loves me unconditionally and my life is based on faith and consciousness, respecting the set of soul contracts that my Spirit wants to experience here on Earth while enjoying life fully.

What I know for sure is that all of us are valuable, unique, divine beings of love and light.

I am committed to impacting at least one billion people on earth, connecting them with the fact that we are of divine essence and that the whole universe conspires to support us on fulfilling our life mission.

If I could get back to those times in the past - years of depression, inner doubt, fear, guilt, and turmoil - I would embrace my past self, telling her while looking into her eyes with a lot of love, appreciation, and gratitude, "You are fine. All is well. Please have faith. Believe in your value and walk into your journey one step at a time, one empowering action, one positive thought, and one smile at a time."

This is my story - the real one, the one that I chose for myself.

What is your story, the one that you tell yourself every day? Is that your truth? Is it the story that you want to live and be known in the world for?

Please reconsider the story you tell to the world, as we are all models in the universe and our story is meant to bring hope and power in the world.

From my heart, to yours, I embrace you with much love and blessings on your journey.

Biography

Danielle Nistor is a Visionary, Messenger and Divine Connector

for the Divine Feminine; a gift that was entrusted to her in the year 2000. During a spiritual pilgrimage, the Divine Mother appeared to Danielle and said to her in that vision, "I want you to be my messenger and bring my divine love and guidance to people."

Since then, in spite of holding a BA in International Law, she decided to dedicate her whole life to spread the messages of healing and divine love.

Danielle is an international inspirational speaker and she leads groups of people to sacred places for healing, transformation, and spiritual evolution. She is also a bestselling writer and the creator of the CD series "Connecting with the Divine".

Danielle also created HealingInSpirit™, a personalized spiritual healing technique that weaves channeling, clearing, healing, and blessing to bring rapid breakthroughs and miracles in people's lives. She has been featured on many radio and television channels internationally.

Her belief is that the universe loves us exactly as we are, that we are valued and unique divine beings of love and light.

A longtime journeyer to sacred places, she invites her life's experiences to continuously re-define and transform her to be able to better serve the people and the Divine. Danielle's life mission is to impact at least one billion people on earth by connecting them with divine love, their own true essence, and their life purpose.

She is committed to truth, self-expression, and respect. She is committed to empower you to shine in your authentic self in order to achieve your life purpose with ease and grace.

Learn More...

Danielle@DanielleNistor.com

http://DanielleNistor.com/

http://www.healingmessagesoflove.com/

https://www.facebook.com/Danielle.Nistor

Joy as a Path to Power
Iris Stallworth-Grayling

You are a spectacular and unique thread in an exquisite tapestry called Humanity! You have been gifted the amazing ability to manifest your destiny and your dreams, which are overflowing with rich harmony and notes that only you can sing. My wish is that my story illuminates more of your path to embrace and express the abundant gifts you already possess. This chapter is an invitation from my heart for you to step out of the shadows as you light up the world with your radiance, wisdom, and power.

My story begins in a recital hall. The audience is waiting, and waiting, and waiting. I can feel the fear gripping my neck, sneaking down my back, and descending into my legs. I feel absolutely terrified! My feet follow the terror, and the next thing I know I am running down the street, tears streaking down my face. I am panicked, embarrassed, and petrified with thoughts of Grandmom's wrath.

This is the first time I run away from the spotlight. I am seven years old.

I run away from the light when I am drenched in the fear of exposing my flaws. There are times that shame and humiliation hold the reins. I steer toward a path that hides the rich color, texture, and intensity of my unique gifts. Does this ever happen to you?

I was raised by a remarkable woman of her times, a 1945 college graduate, an extraordinary accomplishment for any woman and especially a woman of mixed race during this time in history. I picked up a message that came from absorbing her adult words and behaviors, the osmosis of observing life from a young person's lens.

"You must be smart, pretty, and constantly pushing to get ahead."
~ *Iris Beeks Sullivan, (Grandmom)*

This point of reference drove me to believe that my accomplishments were my badge of honor. My value was measured in awards, certificates, and college degrees. My constant sprint to attain success was built on an attachment to the hollow ring of someone else's congratulations. It was empty, because validation came only from the outside in. Fueled by Grandmom's subliminal unspoken messages of never being good enough and never having enough time, I experienced success as a bullet train I was constantly running to catch.

———

Do you have family heirlooms that define and confine you?

———

There was a time when all the pushing caught up with me. I was stressed out and burnt out. The eternal pursuit of the brass ring of success blanketed me with overwhelm and fatigue. The old story began to haunt me. I was too stressed, too busy building a psychotherapy practice, too busy striving to be in my joy.

I hid in full view. I was only revealing the safe and familiar, and seemingly strong, parts of me. Vulnerability was shrouded in a smile and laugh that was a bit too forced. I told myself that I was not enough to step into the light. If I let others really see me, all my flaws would be glowing neon. Again, I was running from the spotlight.

Here's an interesting twist I discovered. It is your vulnerability that connects you to your authenticity. It's when you are joyful and truly yourself that your energy is magnetic. You already possess what it takes to manifest your dreams. This is why, as a Joyologist, it thrills me to my core to share the superpowers of Joy with you.

———

You've been blessed with the divine gift of Joy, which vibrates love, peace, and play. This frequency activates the power to manifest whatever you truly desire!

———

Here's where it gets juicy, awareness crystallizing into focus. I am walking down the steps after a dance class. I remember my to-do list, and the familiar pushing pattern is ignited. I begin to rush. It only takes a nanosecond for old habits to slither in like a snake.

Suddenly, the world is in slow motion. After what seems like a very long time, I hear a loud thump. My face hits concrete! The ER doctor says I'm lucky not to have a major concussion, however I need to recuperate. I am told I must stay in bed for three weeks, resting my body and my brain.

I know deep in my bones that this fall is a defining moment - you know, the ones that are a catalyst for shedding familiar skin so you can stretch into the powerful person you are destined to be.

After the first twelve days of healing in bed, I begin to get into the groove of leaving warp speed behind. I am listening repeatedly to the wisdom of respected teachers and mystics of our times: Deepak Chopra, Abraham Hicks, and Wayne Dyer.

———

"Joy is the divine quality of your true self, which is inherently light-hearted, playful, and free."

~ Deepak Chopra, Spiritual Leader, Integrative Physician

———

These words struck like thunderbolts. Joy is the portal to your authentic expression, which is playful, full of heart, and free of striving. Young children, if they are safe, model this lesson so naturally. At that moment, I realize that Joy is a gift from God, and Joy is a path to power! I am reminded that my thirty-nine years of supporting hundreds of clients to claim their joy and power is a strong foundation on which to build the next phase of my life's work. I have been preparing for this for decades and now is the time to step into my deepest calling as a Joyologist and Manifesting Mentor. This pivotal spark of recognition feels like coming home.

———

Slowing down, observing, expecting miracles, and sharing Joy are keys that open doors to your dream.

———

Joy has three vibrations: Love, Peace, and Play. Each has its unique quality and amazing gift.

1. Love is an exquisite phenomenon that defies definition because it is of the heart, not the mind. It is so primal that we can't thrive without it. Love has many faces: Self-love, divine love, romantic love, and love of all living beings.

2. Another vibration of Joy is Peace, sometimes called quiet Joy. Its characteristics are harmony, balance, and wholeness. Many experience Peace by connecting to the divine or by cultivating a practice of stillness or intentional focus.

3. There is also the Joy of Play which includes laughter, creativity, and sensual delights. We often experience these through exuberant and celebratory expressions of fun.

You are invited to express a harmonious balance of all three vibrations of Joy - Love, Peace, and Play - because this balance is a magnetic energy that uplifts, soothes, and energizes your body, mind, and spirit. I encourage and support you to do this as you serve from the heart, empowering others to thrive.

When you stay connected to the vibrations of Joy, you give to yourself, family, friends, and the world from a replenished cup. If you have put your dreams and desires on the back burner for a long time, they may have become an inaudible whisper. It's your time to be delighted and empowered.

———

Now, it is YOUR time to receive support as you step into your full magnificence! Listen and hear the invitation to come out of hiding so we can revel in the gifts of your greatness.

———

Joy is a potent path to power. From my journey, I have discovered the following powerful manifestation process that I wanted to share with you to help you manifest joy and peace in your life. I invite you to walk through this four-step process. It is deceptively simple. The full potential is achieved with focus, intention, and repetition. Enjoy!

1. Be in a quiet place, slow down, and take three grounding breaths.

2. Close your eyes and bring your dream, your deep desires, into focus with sight/sound/words/emotions (one or more of these is okay).

3. Infuse your dream with the Joy of experiencing your dream.

4. Deepen it by connecting to feeling this Joy in your body. Breathe into your body sensations as if you were living your dream right now. Feeling it in this way energizes your dream so the Universe matches your commitment and co-creates your dream with you.

———

Sharing tools that keep you in the magnetic zone of Joy and Manifestation light me up!

———

I hope my story has touched your life, encouraged you to slow down, tap into your Joy, own your magnificence, and SHINE! I have discovered that as I slow down, tune into my Joy and true self, I more easily shine in my radiance, wisdom, and power. I wish the same for you. I hope you say yes to you, yes to your Joy and yes to your magnificence!

If I can be of any support or you would like to learn additional ways to bring Joy into your life, please go to: www.JoyLovePower.com to tap into additional resources and to get a free gift!

Namaste is a greeting of respect in Hindu culture and this translation beautifully expresses a message that is in my heart: "The light in me bows to the light in you."

May you have a life overflowing with Joy!

Biography

Empress Iris Stallworth-Grayling, LMFT (Ret.), MA, Ct, CPC is a Joyologist, Manifesting Mentor & Transformational Retreat Leader.

As a result of a life-long study of metaphysics and psychology, Iris has been passionate about guiding others to manifest their dreams as they express power from the heart.

Iris had a hypnotherapy practice for twelve years, followed by a thriving clinical psychotherapy practice for twenty-five years. For almost four decades, she was profoundly touched by witnessing hundreds of clients as they claimed their joy and power. Currently, Iris is on a mission to guide women toward living a life full of love, inner peace, and power by supporting them with virtual group programs, individualized VIP coaching, and transformational retreats.

Iris created *The Joy Summit,* an ongoing series of inspirational interviews with those who value Joy as a path to power. She founded The Empowered Empress, a community of powerful, heart-centered women. She has also developed a modality, Expressive Empowering Play, which uses the integrative elements of meditation, dance, and creativity.

Empress Iris is passionate about supporting women who serve from the heart, such as visionaries with a mission, parents, caregivers, teachers, nurses, and healers.

"Elevate your Joy! Energize your Vitality! Manifest your Dreams! You do meaningful work as you support others to thrive, so now is your time to step into the light and shine!"

~ Empress Iris

Learn More...

iris@JoyLovePower.com

www.JoyLovePower.com

https://www.facebook.com/irispowercoaching/

https://www.linkedin.com/in/irisstallworthgrayling

Section 3: You Are Enough!

In this powerful section you will be inspired, encouraged, reminded and discover that you that you are absolutely and truly enough! That you are perfectly equipped and prepared on purpose and with a purpose. Enjoy this inspiring set of chapters as they speak into your soul the truth that you are absolutely enough. As each author shares their story, truths, and powerful actions you can take to help you believe you are enough and in fact needed just as you are! We believe in you and can't wait to see you come out of hiding and SHINE!

Warmly,

Rebecca Hall Gruyter, Book Compiler and Empowerment Leader

Today I GET To ...
Gayle Bode

Life is good today. I get to do so many things, with magnificent people and in a beautiful area. The phrase "I get to" changed my life. That is not how my life started. I thought that there was something wrong with me. People I cared about called me indecisive, flighty, and wishy-washy. They said I was never satisfied and never finished anything. Some of that may have been true. What I know today is that I have a gift.

Looking back, I can see how during my early life, I was drawn into action around guilt, shame, and aggression. Phrases like "you have to" do that in order to be part of the team, event, or even the family would propel me into action or compliance. I heard "what's wrong with you?" and "why are you so stupid?" and "you never appreciate anything." If someone asked me to do something, I always thought I had to do it. Even now, I still struggle to say "no". I thought everyone else's life was more important than mine. I felt I somehow owed them and had to fix things or make up for my imperfections or I felt bad just because I did not already know something.

I remember when I was five years old. My maternal grandfather had just died and soon after we went to the hospital because Uncle Ray was dying also. I know my mom, grandmother, and great-grandmother were very upset - and rightly so. They told me and my older brother, Brad, to sit on the bench that was built into the base of a tree. The bench wrapped all the way around the tree. I am sure my dad or someone else was there with us, but I don't recall who. I thought if I was really, really good and did not move, if I did exactly as they asked, then they would tell me what was going on that made everyone so upset when they came back to get me. I realized recently that part of me was still sitting on that circular bench, waiting for someone to come and tell me it was okay to get up.

For years I was in protective mode. I was always trying to do the right thing at the right time so I would never get in trouble. Growing up, there was a constant double jeopardy and double blinds: you have to do it right the first time, I will show you once, but then you better get it right from then on, and you are not allowed to ask questions. I could not figure it out. This did not add up for someone who loves certainty and order.

I play with numbers because one orange + one orange = two oranges. It is predictable. It is logical. It is safe to get the right answer. No one can dispute that there are two oranges. It can't be misinterpreted or spun off to mean something else.

I see now that I was always looking for safety.

Mental confusion became my defense mechanism. I was waiting to understand better, know more, or be given permission to take my turn. I would have great ideas and visions of things I wanted to do, but I never told anyone. I had a whole world going on in my head.

I developed severe respiratory allergies. I am allergic to forty types of trees and grass and over fifty types of foods, animal, chemical, and environmental toxins, including sterilizing solutions. I have survived anaphylactic shock twice and received permanent medically disabled status. This required me to completely change my career path. It was so severe that I was forced to leave one position and implement an avoidance regime and restrict my environment to only my home for a time. While I still carry an EpiPen (epinephrine auto injector, a.k.a. "bee sting kit") for medical emergencies, I have been able to re-establish my life and career. I am grateful that I rarely consider my disability these days.

In an interesting way, my life has been a series of trying harder to get ahead and then getting pushed back to what seemed like a worse position than before I tried to make a change. One example was when I was in grade school. I dreamed of being a teacher. I had a blackboard in my room and loved to write out my spelling words. I would pretend I was teaching them to my imaginary class. I was sick a lot as a child and often stayed home from school. I really wanted to do well in school, but I did not know I was very allergic to chalk. So the more I studied, the sicker I got.

I had a similar experience after I finished the two-year dental assisting program at San Francisco City College and worked my way up from being a chair-side dental assistant to assisting in maxillofacial dental surgery at Letterman Army Medical Hospital. While I was totally capable of doing the work, I was deathly allergic to the sterilizing solutions. My time in surgery came to an end the day I finished assisting during a surgery, but I had a rash all around my surgical mask on my face and had respiratory distress. I was transferred back to chair-side assisting, but then moved to working in the computerized scheduling system for the entire hospital. Letterman Army Medical Center was considered the Walter Reed Hospital of the west coast. The computer was in its own warehouse and took up half the basement. It was enclosed in glass, temperature regulated, and very loud. I learned to key punch data cards to make changes to the schedule and add patients. I realized that I, too, experience information as data in and data out. It helped me see the big picture and the smallest minute detail all at the same time. My love of processes was born.

My path to accounting began as a job as a receptionist at the Treasury Department. I worked my way up to the secretary to the Regional Director of Human Resources. In learning about writing job descriptions, the inner workings of salary reviews, job reclassifications, and justifications for pay increases, I started to see how jobs and tasks interact. I started to see the relationship between objectives and performances. I was offered a job at a CPA firm that needed an Administrative Manager.

I moved to several different CPA firms as various job offers presented themselves, always working in the Tax Department. While working for a top 10 CPA firm, a new computer program called 123 Lotus came out. This was before Microsoft Excel. I read the entire user manual and created a database for the over 1700 tax returns that could be sorted by various vital pieces of information that the accountants needed, such as due date, fiscal year end date, type of tax return (1040, 1120, 990, or 1065), other related DBA names, children that had their own returns, partnerships waiting on K-1s, and multiple state returns. It was all in there. I found I loved to create systems and see how everything is related.

I joined an organization called AMS, which promotes efficiency in management and participates in research for the purpose of lowering costs, increasing the quality of products, and improving relations between employers and employees. I was on the Board of Directors for four years and became President of the San Francisco Chapter in 1998.

I went to Golden Gate University and studied accounting and business management. I found it very easy to understand and I loved "T" accounts. It all made so much sense to me. I found safety in numbers.

I was working for a large dental office with six doctors who had rotating schedule and multiple offices. At that time, we used manual and handwritten schedules, typed insurance forms, and card ledgers for each patient. The doctors asked me to research and find a new computerized appointment system that would accommodate all the variables of their combined practices. I found a great system and helped implement it in the office.

I thought I had found a way to combine my two years of dental assisting study with my accounting and administrative management skills. What I did not know was that I was developing a severe allergy to the denture and gold crown lab chemicals. While my desk was in the back office, I evidently received enough exposure to cause anaphylactic shock and I left one day in an ambulance, never to return.

Shortly after that incident, my husband of eighteen years left me for his manager at work and had me court ordered out of our home. I was on disability at the time, but I still found a place to live for my two children and myself. My dad gave me his car and I found a new job. I remember the night when I knew my husband was lying to me about his affair. I lay in bed and stopped breathing. Then I thought to myself, "Do I really want to leave my two wonderful children in his care?" The answer was a loud "No." So I chose to start breathing again.

I created Bode Office Solutions in 2009 after being laid off from the construction company where I worked in the accounting department. I provide office management and bookkeeping for entrepreneurs and small businesses.

I can see that all the events, people, places, and situations I have encountered in my life have brought me to the place where I am today.

The phrase "I get to" changed my life. I have always thought about things differently.

Today I know I have a gift to see how things interact and work together. I love to design systems and procedures to make processes more efficient and easier to use. Asking questions, not making quick decisions until I knew what was going on, and seeing both sides of things - the traits that so irritated my parents - are now some of my biggest strengths. Having my own perspective and resilience has helped me so much.

Today, I get to own my own business. I get to set my own hours. I get to do the kind of work I want. I get to spend as much time with my family as possible. I get to to choose how to live my life.

I love to talk to business owners about their operations and accounting systems and help put systems in place. Readers can learn more about my unique view of the business process on my website at http://www.bodeoffice.com.

If I could sit with that little girl waiting on the bench, I would tell her it's safe to get up. It's her turn to cultivate and grow her strengths. I would tell her, "You are creative, tenacious, relentless, resilient, kind, powerful, and caring. Believe in yourself. Trust only trustworthy people. You have a right to have your own life and to live it your way. People will tell you that you owe them or that they are more important than you are. That is simply not true. You get to have your own unique life. It can be no other way. Be valiant! All things are for your good. Go and have a joyful life."

Biography

Gayle Bode began her fascination with the small business financial process when she was eight years old. She loved to look down from the second story windows of their upstairs office and observe how her family's medium-sized grocery store functioned - from stocking the shelves to shopping carts being filled with goods to checking out at the register. Everything was neatly in its place and every location had a function. The freezers kept the frozen food frozen while the fresh produce was up front near the windows for all to see, inviting them to come in. There was order and creativity to the placement of everything. Gayle dreamed of having her own business one day, a very specific type of business - specializing in bookkeeping, accounting, and operations management.

Gayle fulfilled that dream when she became the owner of Bode Office Solutions, providing office management and bookkeeping services in 2009. She has worked in the areas of office management, administrative, and operational management for CPA firms, dental, and chiropractic offices for over twenty-eight years. Gayle helps business owners get more comfortable with their day to day "money IN and money OUT" relationship and have a more realistic conversation around their money without judgment or fear. Gayle specializes in working with holistic healers, auto shops, therapists, architects, and engineers.

Gayle Bode has actively established an experiential lifestyle for herself and her family by overcoming challenges and setbacks and doing more on a regular basis. Gayle makes mental and emotional health a priority while maintaining a sense of curiosity, learning and teaching. To find out more about Gayle, you can go to her website at www.bodeoffice.com.o

Learn More...

gayle@bodeoffice.com

www.bodeoffice.com

www.facebook.com/gayle.bode

Be the Badass Leader of Your Own Life
Sofie Pirkle

Do you know you are a natural leader? It's just that you aren't sure exactly who and where you want to lead and how it will financially support you?

As a blonde-haired, bright green-eyed child, I walked the city streets with the intention of leading the crowds to a new way of being. I danced, twirled, and smiled. My excitement and joy were contagious. I had everyone wanting some of whatever I had.

I am a natural leader and people flocked to me. I was raised in an international self-help and religious organization who taught their believers that its mission was to save the world. The mission, we discovered, was not exactly to benefit the entire world. Well-educated, smart, influential, and deeply caring believers were tricked by the organization's greed.

The most devastating thing and what convinced us to leave (even though we knew we would be considered an enemy if we left) was when we found out that rather than truly helping people, the organization was participating in human trafficking and child sex slavery.

Because of my experience with this organization, I artfully avoided being seen in positions of power and leadership and receiving money as a gifted teacher and community creator. I was terrified that I'd create my own skewed culture without realizing it. After all, I have this master manipulator power to get people to do what I want them to do. My true purpose had been manipulated to make the organization money, and I was terrified of making money off of people even if I was truly helping them. I was terrified of losing my community again.

My work looked successful, but I could not hold on to the money I made. When I would take actions to make more money, my body would shut down as if going against everything I was raised to be. Instead of saving the world in my new, disguised ways, I had to take care of myself first. I hid from everyone to take care of me first.

"Then the day came when the risk to remain tight in a bud," as Anais Nin tells us, "was more painful than the risk it took to blossom."

One day I realized I wasn't special. The art of manipulation is a part of life. Every man, woman, and child practices manipulation in some form consciously as well as unconsciously. The energetic exchange of one's greatest fear or their greatest dream is a slippery affair. In that moment, one person can hand over their power to the other person. It's up to us to consciously recognize it and be aware of our environment. I teach people how to recognize abusive control in their lives, past or present, how they have the power to unintentionally create it, and take action from that awareness.

I know what it feels like to feel like damaged goods, to feel that there is something seriously wrong physically, emotionally, and financially. I also know what it's like to be seen by people in a community who understand where I've come from and how far I have come.

I was amazing at hiding in plain sight. I even put a fake name on my business cards. I believed that I needed to protect my husband, my new family, and my friends.

Although I made up my mind that I wouldn't tell anyone about my cult recovery and religious recovery work, clients who needed my specialized understanding and support were drawn to me.

I know what it feels like to look amazing on the outside, but feel that there must be something seriously wrong with you because no matter what you do, you're not making the money you need to or feeling the way you thought you would. Although you have opportunities to be seen and shine, you manage to side step them or squash the event. Self-sabotage will come in and make it so that you can't speak in the way you want to. You may actually get physically ill. It's okay. You can honor and recognize why those things are happening as a defense mechanism. While you don't have to give in and let it take control completely, there is some part of you that wants to be seen and heard and is freaking out. Often, people think they've done a ton of work and are over it (it being trauma or abuse). But upon going into business, they have to work through those same challenges again in a different way. Many don't make the connection and suffer in silence emotionally and financially.

Interestingly enough, there is a connective tissue between your deep personal work and your business work that demands to be honored, supported, and cultivated always. About 98% is inner work and 2% belongs to outer world. Every part of you has to be in alignment with your inner and outer world strategies. Do not ignore the parts that are screaming. Listen to your body. That's why the cycle of hopping from training to modality to teacher to system usually doesn't work. All of the programs are not necessarily going to be for you and your specific journey. You have to discern what will work for you and trust yourself first. Often we have to stop listening externally and listen to ourselves to get access to the free gift of the mentor inside of you.

In order to be a leader of many, first you must be a leader of one.

Did you know that your brain actually changes when you have been raised in an environment where you are not allowed to trust your own judgment? When your outside world and your inside world don't match, many stop trusting themselves. This can result in feeling like you are going crazy, so the choice is to either not trust yourself or to change your outside environment.

Experience in an abusive environment or psychologically manipulative one can make you not able to shine in the way that you want to. Even though you may have done a lot of healing around this, there is a deeper layer when it comes to attracting the clients you want, the tribe you want, and whatever it is that you say you want financially in your life. If we are not able to be truly ourselves and keep hiding aspects of ourselves, we are likely to never have peace.

We don't need to share everything with everyone, but secrecy is one of the most damaging environments a person can inhabit. Secrecy makes one feel not safe, certainly not accepted, and not truly seen for who we are.

There is a big difference between being visible and being truly seen in our spiritual teaching power. I struggled with "Not Enough" syndrome so I mastered the art of coping with mechanisms that looked healthy, businesses to heal the world, a schedule so full there was no room to think, to feel, to grieve, to feel the underlying terror of the fear that if I was seen in my true leadership power someone, or something, was going to get me.

I became fiercely devoted to showing up for all of the parts of me and having a relationship, especially with my manipulative parts in disguise, the shadowy parts that can hold me hostage. I had to claim all the parts of me in order to connect the dots, to truly help myself and support the people who were coming to me. When I denied any part of myself, it felt like I was cutting off my power. My greatest gifts come from my deepest wounds.

I created support systems all around me to lean into for all the aspects of my life and creating my true identity. I am a spiritual teacher who is divinely compensated in the form of money for my gifts, a mommy to my joy-filled children, and I allow myself to lean into and feel the joy and love that they are. My supportive husband knows I understand exactly what my challenges are, and that the most important thing is for me to go only as fast as the slowest part feels safe to. I am in love with all the parts of my life, and the gems are especially in the hard parts.

Still today, when opportunities present themselves, I sometimes feel physically terrified to not just be visible, but truly seen. My solution is to honor and feel the symptoms, lean into my support systems, and know that part of my journey is to be witnessed as I am, to not hide who I am. I am a Badass Leader AND a Badass Survivor. Both are true. I have the right to cheer from the mountaintops every day for the simple fact that I am alive. Everything else is whipped cream with cherries on top - and I greatly enjoy whipped cream.

The more I hide under my covers, the more capacity I have to shine. When I am not moving forward on something as fast as I want to, I ask myself, "What part of me needs to move slower and be loved right now?" Usually I am due for lounging in my bed. I don't need to transform the world. My presence alone is transformational.

I know I am safe and I can actually feel safe, right now in this moment.

Have you experienced abuse, trauma, tragedy, or toxic environments? Have you seen or experienced abuse of power, extreme manipulation, or even a cult-like experience, and because of that situation vowed to never be that way? Do you sometimes hold yourself back from being in positions of leadership or power or receiving money in those positions?

While you may or may not have struggled with an extreme abusive emotional, spiritual, or physical environment, you may struggle with destructive inner critics or habits that hold you back - fears of success or persecution. You are not alone.

The wisdom I would whisper to my younger self is to slow down, do what you have to do to stop listening to everyone and everything else. Stop and listen to yourself. You cannot truly take care of anyone else if you do not take care of yourself first. Get support and receive it. You are enough. You do enough. You don't need to save the world, or anyone, in any way.

I have supported thousands of clients in their businesses, with their families, world leaders and even those in the entertainment industry as they've struggled with the fear of being seen. There is the fear that pops up (even after many years of effort working through challenges) in the form of their father's voice saying, "you're ripping people off," their mother's voice saying, "you're too much," a former abuser seeing them online or TV and knowing where to find them, or a mob of extremist believers blowing up their community and tribe. The fear is real. The fear needs to be honored.

I've created the Badass Leaders & Survivors Community, where there is understanding community support to safely honor where you come from, protect who you are, inspire where you are going, and most importantly, truly see you for the shining presence you are.

My hope for you is to stop feeling as though there's something wrong with you and to start seeing yourself as someone amazing who won't give up on yourself and your journey.

If you feel safe to connect and share some of your journey with me, or if you're looking for support or resources, such as my From Wounded Healers to Lucrative Badass Leaders program, I would be honored and love to hear from you.

It can feel safe to come out of hiding and shine as yourself. You are the only one made for this job. You are not alone. I invite you to be the Badass Leader of your own life.

Biography

For over two decades, Cult and Trauma Recovery Expert **Sofie Pirkle** has taught thousands of survivors of abuse, trauma, controlling relationships, toxic environments and cults - many who are now Community Leaders, Wounded Healers or Conscious Entrepreneurs - to become Luscious and Lucrative Badass Leaders.

She teaches these courageous and powerful people how to reduce physical and emotional pain and to feel safe, especially in their bank accounts, so they can actually have fun while making their true impact. Feeling their luscious creativity and having lucrative success on their own lounge terms, whether in their families, business, Congress, or Hollywood, her clients go from being Survivors to Badass Leaders.

She is an expert in teaching community leaders and transformational leaders how to create a safe community and culture, discerning subtle differences between a controlling or dependent cult-like environment and an empowering safe culture. Known as their "Canary in the Coal Mine", and "Money Recovery Magic" her clients have recovered from thousands of dollars up to millions of dollars in their businesses, communities, and lives, identifying subtle yet money-sabotaging situations, client repellant, and recognizing financial abuse and exploitation.

A cult survivor herself, Sofie was born and raised in one of the most widely accepted and controversial groups of our modern time: Scientology. Having the courage to escape, heal the soul, and make her true impact, Sofie has a unique knack for working with those who have come from controlling families, abusive relationships, and high demand groups - especially cults.

Sofie understands firsthand how chronic and complex symptoms of post-traumatic stress can range anywhere from mildly irritating to debilitating, how abuse and cult-induced phobias can make even the most confident people terrified of being truly seen, the feelings of feast or famine, self-sabotage, and the unique challenges these very skilled and smart people can have in making and keeping their money.

She is a 5th degree black belt international judge, artistic director of a San Francisco dance company, and bodywork teacher trainer. She has experience in litigation as a translator of cult language and doctrine and in rock climbing the limestone cliffs of Thailand. Sofie makes choices between teaching international governments how to support survivors of human trafficking and child sex slavery and working on leadership projects with highly influential celebrities. She is fiercely devoted to showing up for all of the parts of herself, her clients, and her communities to support them to feel relief, love, and safety while shining and living a luscious and lucrative life on their own terms.

Badass Leaders have the courage to lead their own lives. Whether it's through her books, home study programs, participating in her workshops, or working privately with her, Sofie turns Survivors into Badass Leaders. Sofie's courageous devotion to your journey will touch your heart and ease your soul.

You can find Sofie dancing with her preschool-aged son and baby girl, throwing the occasional tantrum with them, lounging in her cozy bed, and enjoying extra spicy home-cooked Thai food made by her lovely supportive husband of over twelve years in sunny Oakland, CA.

Learn More...

sofie@badassleaders.com

www.badassleaders.com

www.facebook.com/badassleaders

www.facebook.com/Sofie-Pirkle/

May There Always Be Sunshine, Blue Skies and Friendship!
Ana Fatima Costa

One stormy night in late October 1960, my family and I hurriedly left our beloved hilltop home on Madeira Island, Portugal and boarded a ship in the Funchal harbor. After enduring a tumultuous transatlantic voyage, we arrived in New York harbor eleven days later, the week John F. Kennedy was elected President, during a turbulent time in American history. My father excitedly gathered my mother and my four siblings, ages two to thirteen, to look at the Statue of Liberty. Barely seven, I was just happy to be on *terra firma* again. The green statue was meaningless. The last leg of our journey was a three-day train ride ending in Fremont, California, where we lived with distant cousins who owned a dairy farm.

Two years later, Papa had saved enough to buy a plot of land in East Oakland, California with a two-bedroom, one-bath house. It was too small to accommodate our family of seven, so he built a three-bedroom, one-bath house in the spacious backyard. We moved into the modern home, and Papa's two older sisters moved into the older one.

The first twelve years on this foreign land were difficult. Our previous life was idyllic, filled with family, friends, and abundance. Now, we lived in a harsh environment, where we needed to learn a new language and culture and how to survive. Mama forbade us from stepping beyond our driveway except to go to school or the corner market.

At school, kids taunted our speech, dress, and food, but the biggest adjustment was the violence in our neighborhood and in the nation: the murders of John F. Kennedy, Malcolm X, Martin Luther King, Jr., and Bobby Kennedy. Plus, there was also the civil rights riots and Vietnam War.

As a child, I silently mourned the loss of my friends and home in Funchal and could not comprehend why we left. I learned later that because of Papa's work as a journalist, dictator Antonio Salazar had threatened his life because he wouldn't play by the rules. Now Papa had a weekly radio show, *Amigos de Portugal*, where the First Amendment allowed him to speak freely and without fear.

Television transformed my life. I learned how to meditate watching *Lilias, Yoga and You*. I fell in love with the drama of the courtroom scenes in *Perry Mason* and decided to become a court reporter.

1983 was a transformative year. Four years into my career, I was earning a good living doing what I loved, and I had a rich social life. I also enjoyed drawing, belly dancing, massage, and singing classes. For the first time since Portugal, I was happy.

Yet there were aspects of my life that I held close to my heart: my spiritual practices and deepest beliefs. Only my closest friends knew that I meditated every day, kept a dream journal, was in a crystal healing class, had Reiki sessions, consulted tarot cards, participated in shamanic journeys, studied and used alternative healing modalities in lieu of Western Medicine, smudged myself and my home with white sage and other sacred herbs to release negative energy, read dozens of books about spirituality, and experimented with mind-altering substances.

The irony of working in the legal field while using illegal drugs was not lost on me, but I rationalized that as long as my actions did not negatively impact my work or anyone else, it was no one's business. Cannabis and psilocybin helped me to release stress, connect with nature and my body, open my heart, and see things from another person's point of view, especially when there was conflict. Had they known about it, my legal colleagues may have questioned my involvement in these esoteric practices. But one day, I had an experience that changed everything.

During a self-guided visualization in September 1983, I opened a door leading to a manifestation room, and instead of seeing something that I wanted to bring into my life, a faceless woman wearing a nurse's uniform stood on the other side of the threshold and handed me a baby wrapped in a blue blanket. My body jolted back from the shock, and I slammed the door shut. The vision disappeared as I opened my eyes for a moment to get my bearings. Then I closed them again, trying to shut out the memory. Wrapping my arms around my legs, I rocked myself back and forth in a seated position and moaned, "No, no, NO! Not now! Please, God, not a baby! Not yet. I am not ready! I do not want to manifest *a baby* just when I am feeling in control of my life."

Seven years previously, I had given up a child for adoption and promised myself that the next time I got pregnant, I would do it right – after I was happily married to my soulmate. I was dating someone who could possibly be that person, but it was too early to know.

My mother is deeply intuitive. She has known things that no one told her. And I have had premonitions and dreams come true. I couldn't shake off the vision.

True enough, in the light of a late December waning gibbous moon, my lover and I were surrounded by an otherworldly glow that emanated love, what can be best described as an angelic experience. When we awoke later that morning, I knew that I was pregnant.

Things started to escalate. In February 1984, my partner called, his usual subdued voice exuding enthusiasm. All he revealed was that he wanted to ask me something, and it was important. During the three hours it took for him to drive from Mendocino, I busied myself to keep from pacing. I prepared dinner, cleaned house, and did laundry.

When I opened the door, Jerry was all smiles, looking like he could barely contain himself. He kissed and hugged me briefly, then took my hands and led me to my futon.

"What's going on, Jerry? What's so important that you drove three hours to see me?"

"Something happened during one of my meditations a few days ago. I was sitting, focusing on my breath, as I always do, and saw in my mind's eye some dolphins leaping in the ocean...off the coast of Russia." He stopped for a moment, watching to see if I was with him.

"Okay. Go on."

"Then I saw a man and a woman, American citizens, traveling to the Soviet Union. The woman is pregnant and gives birth on the steps of the Kremlin."

"What?"

His words tumbled out with excitement. "Well, not literally. This was a vision, you see? It hit me like a lightning bolt. A baby born to American citizens in the Soviet Union would be a living bridge of peace between the two nations involved in the Cold War. And dolphins were jumping out of the sea nearby in joy."

Jerry took a long deep breath, his eyes locked on mine. "How would you feel about giving birth to our baby in the Soviet Union?"

There it was. I immediately visualized an elderly woman in a gray overcoat, a colorful babushka scarf covering her head and shoulders, resolutely bracing against a cold wind.

Then I closed my eyes and drifted ...

Throughout my American education, history seemed to be mostly about conquering others. From the time that Columbus had "discovered" America, I had wanted to know more about the Native people's culture, beliefs, and values. Victors write the history, so textbooks are written from their viewpoint. I wanted the complete truth.

In a 1983 speech, President Reagan had proclaimed the Soviet Union the "Evil Empire." He quoted a 1920 Lenin lecture that the USSR repudiated all morality that proceeds from "supernatural" ideas. Reagan believed that meant the Soviets don't believe in God; thus, they are enveloped in darkness and cannot be trusted.

When I heard his interpretation, I felt an overwhelming sense of foreboding. Since the beginning of time, hasn't mankind killed in the name of God? Hasn't the U.S. engaged in actions that could be judged as evil by others around the world - dropping atom bombs in Hiroshima and Nagasaki, for example?

I had begun to wonder if the anti-Soviet messages and images that were being transmitted through the media were purposefully generated to create fear in the American people in order to fuel the concept of war as the only option to respond to behaviors we cannot tolerate. Using the phrase "peace through strength" and calling a missile that can kill or maim "The Peacekeeper" sounded like oxymora to me.

Yet, I am not political. Traditionally, politicians appear to say the same things – different party, different suit, different face, same words. Traditionally, I vote for whom I think is the "lesser of two evils" and hope that the candidate I chose doesn't do more harm than the previous president.

My own personal life is filled with plenty of obstacles and concerns to keep me busy, so I put those things aside over which I have no control and live my life, doing my best to do the right thing in my day-to-day world.

Yet the inflammatory rhetoric being flung back and forth across the Atlantic was worrisome. Cartoonist Walt Kelly once wrote in his comic strip *Pogo,* referring to the turmoil caused by the Vietnam War, *"We have seen the enemy, and they are us."*

Each of us has the capacity to hurt others. As an imperfect being, I certainly have. Maybe if we all act with kindness and try to listen to and understand one another, there wouldn't be any enemies.

I was beginning to wonder if maybe the Soviet people were *not* our enemy. Aren't they just like us, wanting the same things we want: food, shelter, health, enough money to pay their bills, time with their families, and enjoyment of life? Maybe the simple human act of traveling across the globe and entrusting the Soviet people with the birth of our baby on their land would help bridge this frightening impasse between the two nations in a small way.

I exhaled and opened my eyes. It felt like an eternity since Jerry had asked me, but in reality it was about a minute. "Okay, Jerry. I don't know much about politics or history or government, but I do want peace, and for whatever reason this is happening, I trust in our visions and in my guidance and intuition. I have no idea how to make something like this happen, but if it's going to help bring peace to our world, then let's do it."

The next six months flew. Jerry moved in with me, and we got married. We made preparations for our trip: secured a loan, ordered passports and visas, mapped our journey, spoke with people familiar with travel and communications within the USSR, and myriad other tasks. Throughout the entire time, profound, synchronistic, spiritual "coincidences" intensified. Despite my own fears and our families' worries, I trusted Spirit's guidance every step of the way.

In late August 1984, Jerry and I boarded a plane in San Francisco when I was eight months pregnant, and we traveled 5500 miles by air, sea, and land to Leningrad, where our baby Alexander (nicknamed Sasha) was born in our hotel room on September 6th. A Soviet journalist who "happened" to be visiting our hotel during the birth published an article about our mission and the news spread like wildfire. The media christened Sasha "The Peace Baby."

The Soviet people showered us with love, gratitude, gifts, and hundreds of letters, cards, photographs, drawings, and telegrams. Most of the handwritten letters were in Cyrillic and contained similar sentiments: "We want no war! May there always be sunshine, blue skies, and friendship!"

One letter in English stood out. Svetlana, 20 and pregnant, wrote that she and her husband worried about the threat of nuclear war. "Let us hope that our sons will never send death to each other."

Amen.

Biography

For as long as I can remember, before I make a wish - while blowing out candles on a birthday cake or throwing coins in a fountain - I "hear" three words as soon as I close my eyes: Peace. On. Earth.

Yet my personal life has been anything but peaceful.

As a court reporter, I learned how to detach from the emotion, politics, and drama of lawyers and witnesses at a deposition or trial while simultaneously detaching from my own internal reactions to the intensity - no matter what I heard and how I felt about it. Although I understood what feelings were intellectually, I had difficulty expressing my own. And needs? No idea. This ignorance resulted in several damaged relationships and three divorces. While my career was going well, my personal life was a mess.

Years later, during my training to become a Connection Practice coach, I learned that the foundation of all human conflict manifests from sensations (i.e., feelings) that arise in us when we have unmet needs. When we're faced with an emotional situation, the amygdala (a.k.a. the "reptilian" part of the brain) generates the "fight or flight" response faster than we can think. Based on past information and events, it keeps us trapped in negative emotional patterns, and we tend to overreact to situations. In the extreme, violence may result. These patterns can lead to stress, heart disease, and other health challenges and prevent us from experiencing happiness.

One day while coaching highly intelligent, educated professionals during a group practice session and observing them struggle to grasp this new communication style, I had a flash of insight: *All human behavior is based on universal feelings and needs, and we act consciously or unconsciously to meet those needs.*

But understanding our own feelings and needs and communicating them calmly is hard work! It's a new language that is not easy to master. Yet when we become more aware of our own feelings and needs, we are more open to truly listening and responding to others' feelings and needs. I finally understand that living a life in harmony with others is only possible when I am at peace with myself *first*. Maintaining this harmonious state requires self-compassion and self-awareness. And now, most days, I am at peace. At last.

The above chapter is based on my forthcoming book, *Labor of Love: My Journey Through the Iron Curtain to Birth the Peace Baby.*

Learn More...

ana@anafatimacosta.com

www.anafatimacosta.com

https://www.facebook.com/anafatimacostaconsulting/

https://www.linkedin.com/in/anafcosta

We Are All Designed to Shine
Trisha Garrett

Unforeseen Darkness

It was a time of quiet celebration. The atmosphere was full of a joyful anticipation of something wonderful about to happen. Then, without any warning, there were unforeseen complications and tragedy struck. My mother and her baby died while she was giving birth. Instead of celebration, there was mourning.

Total stillness was in the air, a disruptive silence that consumed the room and which even my tiny two-year-old body could feel. I vaguely remember an undercurrent of confusion and embracing the silence as I longed for the comfort of a mother that I would never kiss, hug, or touch again. I would never experience her smile or hear her sweet spirit say "I love you". She would never teach me about the birds and the bees or show me how to put on makeup. The loss of my mother and the secret details surrounding her death would send me on a journey of discovering that I am truly designed to shine.

As I grew older, I had so many questions surrounding my mother's death, I learned very quickly that this topic was off limits in my family. If I did stir up the nerve to bring it up, there would suddenly be this elephant in the room that everyone would shy away from. I did not understand why it was a secret. This was my mother and I had a right to know everything, even what she liked and what made her laugh. I was so young that I did not have the language to express the deep feelings of grief, shame, embarrassment, and an underlying feeling that something was wrong with me. Growing up without a mother and being unable to explain the circumstances around her death began to fester, casting a grey film of grief and emotional turmoil that overshadowed my life for years to come.

Mommy Dearest

At around five years old, a family member named Sharon and her daughter came to live with us to help my father. Little did I know that Sharon's oppressive spirit would feed into the internal grey film that was festering, eating at my wounded soul, adding depth to the darkness. It manifested itself in self-doubt, a host of insecurities, and feelings of not being enough in a quest for unattainable perfection. Sharon had a way of making me feel like I was insignificant, like I was always doing something wrong or that there was something wrong with me. When there was something I enjoyed, she had a way of turning it around and making me feel badly about myself. It seemed to bring her pleasure to see me experience the emotional pain. I could never please her.

I remember having fun playing outside with the neighborhood kids at about eight years old. I looked up and Sharon and her daughter, who was eight years older than me, were headed for the car. I wanted to go, so I excitedly ran over to Sharon and bravely asked if I could go too. She looked at me with a smirk on her face and said, "Look at you – you're filthy! Look at your hair – it's a mess! Why would I want to take you with me looking like that?" I was embarrassed. I had hoped for a different outcome; however, I had grown accustomed to being met with criticism. Sharon was my Mommy Dearest.

Thinking fast on my feet and holding the tears back, I sheepishly asked, "I can run inside and clean up really fast?" Sharon looked down at me and said, "I am leaving now. I am not waiting for you. You should not have gotten so dirty." As she continued to walk to the car, I kept trying to convince her that I could clean up quickly. Now getting into the car, she turned to me, pointing her finger in my face, and said, "I am not waiting and you're not going."

My heart sank; my bravery diminished. I cried internal tears with my heart aching, feeling confused and rejected. Her negative attitude and critical words were starting to take over my mind. Maybe I should not have been playing outside, but I really liked playing with my friends. I just had to remember to stay clean. Maybe next time she would let me go. Darkness continued to grow. My world began to shrink as I strived for perfection. I continued to box myself in more and more over the years. I was looking for acceptance and unconditional love - a mother's love. Instead, I was met with criticism, shame, and emotional embarrassment from my caretaker.

Hiding in Self-Doubt

As a teenager, my self-doubt was massive. I was taking less risks because I was fearful of making mistakes. My life was extremely dark with only glimmers of light. Looking for relief from my inner pain, I unconsciously turned to food, which began a cycle of binging and purging with laxatives, a cycle that would last for years.

Initially, I felt like I was totally in control of my bulimia, binging and purging only when I chose. It was my secret and I took pride in making sure that no one knew. Over time, it became a normal ritual for dealing with my emotions. I had so many constant triggers. My caretaker's voice of criticism was replaced with my own internal voice, which never slept. My sense of what was normal no longer existed. What started out as a way to have relief and comfort turned into more shame and guilt as the craving to binge and purge began to run my life. It became an addictive cycle that seemed to have no ending. I was physically destroying my body and the guilt was eating away at me. I wanted to stop, but how could I stop? The bulimia had me; I did not have it. It only provided a temporary unhealthy comfort. I was no longer in control. However, on the outside things were looking great.

As I navigated through my days in my mid-20s, the emotional pain was still unconsciously feeding that dark space within me. My light to shine was barely functioning. Feeling alone, I was dying inside, though outwardly I pretended to smile. I had wonderful friends, I was active in my church, and I had a great job with a major corporation. How much better could things be? No one knew the deep, conflicting, tormenting pain that I felt. A constant undertone of feeling that I was not enough was well-nourished by my insecurities. No matter what goal I accomplished, I never learned to celebrate myself. I would still doubt myself. I had major issues with body image. I could not imagine anyone really loving me. I was dying a slow death inside and out. I didn't want to continue to hurt myself. I just wanted the pain to stop! Was it really possible to be happy? I believed it was for others but not sure true happiness was available for me.

Coming Out

Now in my 30's, I finally discovered that true happiness was available for me too. Embracing who God has designed me to be and with the support of friends, I stopped binging and purging. After a time of reflection, I learned that I did not have to be afraid of "it", whatever "it" was holding me back. Feeling empowered, I saw light at the end of the tunnel. I realized that no matter how my life started, change is possible for me. Once I became conscious of the shame, hurt, and embarrassment, I did not have to carry it. Facing the painful tragedy of my mother's death, I released it to God. The film of grey began to lighten as I looked at myself in the mirror. I smiled and it was real in that moment.

Coming out of hiding was a process that has taken many years and I am still learning to shine brighter. One major turning point was when I decided to believe and trust in God. Over time, I accepted the fact that even if no one else loved me, God loved me. Most importantly, God loved me unconditionally and there was no pressure to be perfect!

What was once a small glimmer of light is now bursting through, decimating the darkness, and restoring my sense of bravery. Once the binging and purging stopped, the emotional scars had to be addressed. I found a doctor that began to treat me holistically. I was met with warmth and no judgment. The doctor was just as concerned with my physical well-being as my emotional well-being. With every step forward, my courage grew. I shared with a small circle of friends and they were extremely supportive.

Several years later I was unhappy in my job, but too fearful to make a change. Finally, an exciting temporary opportunity came my way and I wanted it. However, there was a major obstacle. My Senior VP was not going to hold my current position, which meant that in three months, I could potentially be without a job. This time instead of shrinking, something rose up within me. It felt like the heavens opened up, shining brightly. Nervous and excited at the same time, one step at a time, I decided to trust in me, believe in me, take a risk on me. I accepted the temporary position. I cried out loud and smiled inside. That decision changed the course of my life, which put me on my current path.

Journey to Shine

I have always had a desire to enrich the lives of others, each action allowing me to shine brighter. Taking baby steps, my transformation started as I worked with toddlers in a very large church I attended. Babies are so forgiving. I didn't have to be perfect; just loving.

I have headed professional development conferences and worked with several non-profit organizations over the years. However, one of the most powerful life changing programs, for me, has been Motivating the Teen Spirit. A safe space is created so teens can take responsibility for their actions, fall in love with themselves, and know that they are not alone. As the teens are being served, it feeds my soul to witness their transformation and that of their families. Coaching a client to take that courageous baby step so that they can shine brighter is my passion. I literally help them come out of hiding and shine. Now as a transformational life coach, I desire to continue to help as many people as possible to come out of hiding so that they can live their best life and shine.

Here are a few tips I would like to share to help you come out of hiding to shine:

1. Develop a strong spiritual practice where you will find unconditional love to help you move forward.

2. Be patient and kind to yourself. Take baby steps…it's a journey.

3. Forgive yourself and others that have hurt you so that you can heal.

4. Get the support you need throughout your journey. Surround yourself with people that see your greatness and can love you through the pain.

5. Believe in yourself. You are designed to shine!

6. Enjoy the journey and remember to celebrate!

We are all designed to shine, and I want to encourage you on your journey as you are stepping forward. If you would like support by conversation, I would love to connect with you. I would like to celebrate with you how this chapter touched you because YOU are designed to shine. It has been healing and an honor to share my story with you. We are victorious and wonderfully made to SHINE with a purpose!

Biography

Trisha Garrett is the Founder and Owner of Trimiah Coaching and Consulting. Her professional career began over eighteen years ago when she worked for Fortune 100 companies in the Silicon Valley. She held various positions over the years including Executive Assistant, Onboarding Manager, Corporate Internal Life Coach, and Business Operations Analyst. In all of these roles, she had a consistent passion to impact so many lives. Trisha worked on groundbreaking efforts in education, environmental initiatives, and government and community outreach.

A hunger and purpose to help women stand up, live bigger, and thrive deepened as she refined her coaching craft. Donating her time to a non-profit organization is a great example. Trisha headed up the mentoring and coaching program. Throughout her time with the organization, she trained new mentors and provided educational, career, and life coaching for single mothers.

Core to her passion, for several years Trisha led Girl's Technology Day at Intel Corporation. The purpose of the annual event was to introduce, stimulate, and encourage African American and Latino girls from underserved communities interest in Science, Technology, Engineering, and Math (STEM) careers.

Trisha is a Certified Professional Co-Active Coach (CPCC) receiving training from Coach Training Institute (CTI); where she also received a Certification in Leadership. As one of the most rigorous, oldest, and largest in-person coach training organization in the industry, CTI is also accredited by the International Coaching Federation (ICF). She has a Bachelor of Science in Business Administration and a Marketing Certification. She has trained with Motivating the Teen Spirit and she is certified in Predictive Index Assessments (personality assessment). She received a Certification of Completion in Urban Youth Yoga & Mindfulness training.

Trisha is very passionate about helping people move to the next level of living by standing up, being courageous in designing a bold, exciting, bigger life, and thriving!

Learn More...

trimiahcoachingandconsulting@outlook.com

www.trimiahcoachingandconsulting.com

www.facebook.com/groups/trimiahcoachingandconsulting/

www.twitter.com/TrimiahCC

It's Your Time and Your Turn - Be Seen, Heard, and Celebrated!
Dr. Anita M. Jackson

Psychology tells us that within our human development is a deep need and desire for love, belonging, and safety. This need often and unconsciously influences how we allow ourselves to be seen, heard, celebrated, interacted with, and experienced whether with ourselves, others, or with life itself. When these needs are met, we have the potential of living a more balanced life while feeling more fulfilled, satisfied, complete, and energized, which can help us enjoy and navigate the beauty of life in all its complexities. And yet the opposite is just as true. If these needs are not met (love, belonging, and safety), our subconscious mind, or our ego, convinces us to believe that we need to "protect" ourselves from the possibility of being hurt, rejected, abandoned, or anything else that threatens our very existence. In its love for us, our subconscious mind feels it needs to do whatever necessary to keep us alive, and yet ironically, in keeping us alive, it can cause us to hide.

"Coming out of hiding and shining", at its core, means to finally allow ourselves to fully be seen, heard, and celebrated without shame, guilt, fear, or apology. To fully come alive, it starts with an awareness that one has been "asleep" or unconscious to our divine nature and truth, or the very idea that there is the potential for so much more in our personal lives and business. For me, my first wave of coming awake, alive, or out of hiding started when I received my doctorate on 7/7/2007, which I think is pretty significant, and it started the downward spiral effect of transformation, re-identification, rebranding, and up-leveling to my new calling and purpose in life. This transformational process happens to all of us who are called to **more**, which means **YOU**!

I remember it very clearly. After celebrating yet another degree with my family and going home to my new, but empty, house, I remember thinking, "What's next?" You see, for years, I had allowed myself to pursue my education and career, believing that it would give me the value, meaning, and purpose I desperately longed for and needed because childhood experiences had directly and indirectly convinced me to believe that I wasn't good enough.

Immediately after asking my question of "what's next", I heard my spirit say, "It didn't do what you thought it would do, did it?" Meaning, all my hard work didn't bring about more value, meaning, or purpose that I desired. Those things are not, and never have been, based on "doing", but in my/our "being-ness". Being is based on remembering that our wholeness is comprised of our divinity and humanity working together for the full allowance and experience of present moment feelings, thoughts, and behaviors. **BUT,** when we are asleep or hiding, "being" is almost impossible. Instead, "hiding" makes us dysfunctional, separated, and closed off from our true nature as one with God as Source, the Universe, and spiritual truths which ultimately causes us to unconsciously seek outside ways to feel whole, complete, fulfilled, satisfied, abundant, wealthy, and healthy with everything else that we were divinely created for as our birthright. Like most of us and as stated above, when love, belonging, and safety are not fully experienced, our perception of who we are, how we show up, and our interactions with ourselves, life, and others shapes our ongoing condition to living life with purpose and meaning.

As a Success Transformational Coach working mostly with women, the top three challenges I see with most of my clients is their struggle with not feeling good enough, visibility, and money (which I strongly, personally believe is directly linked to our overall sense of self value, worth, and the ability to receive, or lack thereof). This challenge, in a very slight and subtle way (and sometimes in a very direct way), shuts us down or causes us to hide. Hiding, at its core, is the idea of "keeping a secret" or to "conceal someone or something from discovery." On a more personal level, hiding is the act of holding back our true spiritual authenticity, our gifts, talents, abilities, dreams, and desires for fear that they are unrealistic, improbable, and unattainable as well as thinking we will be judged and rejected because of having them. Ultimately, this causes us to "go with the flow", "do what's expected of us", work hard...or just exist.

Signs You're Hiding

There are very clear telltale signs indicating that we are in hiding, and until we become aware and recognize that we are living under such false truths, we cheat ourselves out of the opportunity to experience our divine birthright in love, belonging, safety, and abundance. Here are just a few indicators that you might be in hiding:

- Dissatisfied or unfulfilled in all or most areas of your life

- Easily distracted or bored

- Busy but not productive

- Financial struggles

- Spiritually unsettled or disconnected from God, Source, or Spirit

- Mental or emotional imbalance (frustrated, confused, anxious, depressed, worried, lack mentality, etc.)

- Problems with trust, relationship, health, etc.

- Body image issues (includes weight problems)

- Closed or disconnected from sexuality and sensuality (can come from experiences of various types of abuse)

These indicators are not given to cast guilt or judgment, but to hopefully cause you to take a serious look at where you are in your life and the decisions (reach a definite conclusion within yourself) you might need to make in order to wake up and come out of hiding. And here's what I know to be absolutely true because of my very own experiences: if we are in hiding (whether consciously or unconsciously), God and life have a very interesting way of shifting you around and turning everything upside down in order to get your attention and pull you out of hiding to shine in the magnificence of who you were created to be. Everything works together for your highest and most perfect good – even the pain!

My second wave (because I'm slightly stubborn and hardheaded) of my coming out of hiding journey began in June 2011 when I was laid off from my lucrative dysfunctional, but safe job. From there I experienced a whirlwind of transitions, several losses, confusion, and confrontation with my own truth that unveiled that there was/is something more for me and my purpose than just barely, merely existing. I now declare that each wave of coming out of hiding was - and still is - the best thing that ever happened to me, however, I didn't really start feeling that way until 2015. Up until that point, there were a few other experiences that I needed to have in order to understand the power of my being me (authentic), being visible, and allowing myself to shine in the fulfillment of my destiny and purpose.

In 2013, I was gifted the opportunity to go to Hawaii and speak at a weeklong conference. It was the first event where all of my expenses were paid to speak, so I was very happy to attend. While there, we were given a day off to explore the island. We chose to visit Diamondhead, which is Hawaii's Rainforest. As we walked through this amazing "jungle," we came across a clearing that, in my mind, looked like the Garden of Eden. From where I was standing, the scenery was breathtaking. I was really taken by the view, feeling a "pull" to just be still and present to the surroundings. Well, without going into all the extreme details, while taking in the scenery, I quietly heard, "Anita, you're not being who we created you to be." Of course this caused a series of questions and statements, all in defense of my believing that I was being exactly who I thought I was created to be, and yet, deep inside I knew that wasn't exactly true.

You see, as a young child I was very attracted to being a "celebrity" - not like the ones you see in Hollywood, but a celebrity who is a feminine, powerful, successful, a multi-millionaire who is a strong, influential role model to others in being and living a life that is the absolute fullest of truth and abundance in every sense of the word. And, although my background and environment stated I could do good and have nice things, it indirectly stated that I couldn't want more than what I already had. Instead, I misinterpreted, as any child would, that I must work hard for everything I wanted, and that being too rich would make me susceptible to ruin. So I did what was acceptable and required of me, all the while constantly feeling as if something was wrong, off, and missing. This "something is missing" feeling constantly haunted me. However, I had become convinced that it was just me and I could never tell anyone that I secretly desired...MORE. As a side note, please understand that our desire for "more" in life is the yearning of essence, Spirit, and God's way of fully being expressed and realized in us and through us. We were created with an innate desire to grow and expand ourselves and when this is not done or allowed, we feel dissatisfied, unfulfilled, or empty. Interestingly enough, these and other emotions can cause us to hide, creating the perpetual vicious cycle of longing, lack, and dysfunction.

It's Your Time and Turn to Come Out and Shine

There has never been a more perfect time than now for any person, and especially for women, to come out of hiding and shine. Why? Because despite all the amazing things that we as women have done individually and collectively, there is still so much more for us to do in reconnecting and reclaiming our spiritual sense of being-ness, restoring our family connection and legacy, rebuilding our moral and ethical character foundation, and establishing financial security, independence, and freedom that can bring about the tipping point of universal unlimited success in every aspect of living life.

To make this a truth for us, we need to make a committed decision to "become" our highest and unlimited best, do the work within us and before us without fear, and recognize that our unlimited and outrageous success is, and always has been, done in relationship with God, ourselves, and others – in that order...ALWAYS. May you hear this truth deep within your spirit, heart, soul, and mind and then never stop moving and living forward.

To Your Unlimited and Outrageous Success ~ Dr. Anita M. Jackson

Biography

Dr. Anita Jackson is the Founder and CEO of The Unlimited Woman Lifestyle & Business Network and AMJ Productions and Publications. She is also the Sr. Executive Producer of Outrageous Success Women's Network Channel (powered by VoiceAmerica Network) and produces other online TV shows promoting the empowerment and success of women around the world. Through AMJ Productions and Publications, she is the publisher of *I Am Enough* Magazine, an international online magazine, and feminine empowerment lifestyle, luxury magazine *The Unlimited Woman* (publishing 2017).

And finally, she is the #1 bestselling author of her own book, *Becoming Outrageously Successful: A Woman's Guide to Finding Her Purpose, Fueling Her Passion and Unlocking Her Prosperity*. She is a co-author in three additional bestselling books and is currently writing in two other books, one as compiler and the other as a co-author.

With twenty-five years of experience in personal and business psychotherapy, Dr. Anita works with women worldwide to deeply and profoundly reach their highest and fullest potential while reaching outrageous success in their personal life and business.

Learn More...

www.dranitamjackson.com

dranita@dranitamjackson.com

www.oswtv.com

www.iamenoughmagazine.com

Finding My Tribe
Jacquie Farquhar

The day my father left created a huge hole in my heart. I found it hard to speak about it for years to come, and I believed keeping the news a secret would protect me from the shame of divorce. Divorce was more of a stigma in those days when most parents stayed together, if even for the sake of the family. The security of our family became replaced with a sense of embarrassment, but the shell I created around me just kept the hurt closer as my loneliness grew. The family I knew had disintegrated before my shell-shocked eyes.

I escaped from my emotional pain by diving into books and I developed into a voracious reader. Fiction of all kinds appealed to me, allowing me to escape into the pages of other characters' stories. People thought I was hiding behind cracked covers and dog-eared pages while in reality, I was finding my salvation. To this day, books are my constant companions. I always have a book in my purse and I read every night before bed. The words on the page relax me, allay my anxieties, and allow my spirit to find a consistent place to rest and rejuvenate.

My family and I picked up the pieces the best we could and coped with the new future ahead of us as well as could be expected. From this, I learned to help my family and myself. After school, I went home to cook dinner for my siblings and do my homework before bed. There wasn't much room for me to just be a kid. Self-sufficiency came naturally to me as I adapted to the drastic shifts in my family life. These unwelcomed changes also made me stronger and more resourceful. I babysat until I was old enough to work to avoid being more of a financial burden to my mother than I had to be while she worked and went to school. She was an inspiration, a single mom with six children who completed her Ph.D.

As I got a little older, my family went on a summer camping trip to an island in the middle of a large lake in Canada. When we were packing up to leave the island, Dad decided it was my job to drive the boat half a mile across a foggy lake to pick up my siblings, knowing I had never driven the boat before. He quickly showed me how to use the motor and told me to yell if I got lost. Pointing me in the general direction of the island, he told me not to veer too far, lest I go over the dam. I was scared because it was something new to me and I couldn't see very far through the fog. The one thing I did know was that I could do it. It never crossed my mind that I would fail because my father believed in me. I steered my way through the thick fog and had to stop a few times to call out to them, but I finally reached the shore and got them safely back to the side where our father was waiting. From then on, I knew I could do anything I set my mind to. There are times in life when I forget this lesson, but then I remember this story and know that I am strong and capable.

At the age of twenty, I married a cheater. It was a short-lived, volatile relationship. When it ended, I resolved never to repeat that experience again. I had suffered enough emotional trauma already and there would be no room for any more in future relationships. Divorced by the age of twenty-three, I realized I didn't need someone else to complete me. Single again, I learned to stand on my own two feet once more.

I released myself from any expectation of finding a new partner and I turned my focus toward work. I learned the ins and outs of the hospitality industry, managing the banquet services for larger and larger gatherings. It gave me great joy to bring the disparate pieces of a puzzle together to form the final picture of a client's event. Doing this, I began to receive recognition for my gifts. I was being seen for my contributions.

My shyness faded away and an inherent calling to be of service shone brightly through me.

I worked hard and still, I felt there was something missing. My innate traveler's spirit moved me from Colorado to Nevada to Wisconsin to California. At last, I found new opportunities, and they led me to my life's greatest gift, my daughter, that I had with my second husband. Keeping her safe and well cared for became my sole purpose. From the moment she was born, my spirit connected with hers and together we rode a wave of hard times through divorce, bankruptcy, and the loss of my father. Despite the hardships, we have lived well because we loved and supported each other and lifted each other up when life would drag us down.

Without my daughter to anchor me in moving forward, at the age of fifty, I would have given in to a total collapse of spirit. The life I had built as an adult was falling apart around me, my work/life fulfillment dissolved, and my body changed in ways I did not expect. I realized I was being overlooked. Again

As a teen, I had been heavy. When I lost weight in my 20's, people noticed me, they paid more attention to me, as if all of a sudden I had more value because of the way I looked. The one thing I could count on throughout my 20's, 30's, and 40's was my vitality. As my physical energy began to wane at menopause, a depression settled into my bones. I gained weight and started disappearing from people's radar. I was being treated as if I were invisible again. Even though I was the same person, I was being devalued based on my looks by those around me. The experience rattled my cage, shook my foundation, and in the end, woke me to a revived sense of myself.

In 2009, I was introduced to the realm of holistic practices, which opened my eyes to an entirely new way of being. From this new perspective, I chose to study to become a life coach. I learned that I didn't need a college degree to move forward in ways that were meaningful to me. I realized my life education was infinitely bigger than I thought it had been. The despair I had felt as a child and young adult didn't have to darken my experience as a wise woman of the world. An epiphany struck me: life could be different if I chose for it to be different. I said aloud to myself, "My thoughts create my life."

Life coaching also taught me self-care practices, like making sure I have time for myself each day, reading one of my beloved books for fifteen minutes to shift my energy, stopping to do a ten minute meditation, or using my weekends to go to the beach where my soul lights up. I also learned that holistic care includes the relationships we engage in, personally and professionally. In so many ways, this helped me grow into the person I am today.

I didn't have a lot of money, so I volunteered at the personal development seminars and workshops that I wanted to attend. I felt lifted into the light of my gifts as a person of integrity, clarity, and compassion. I had found my passion in life. One of my biggest lessons from these events was that not even in communities of shared purpose is everyone operating on the same vibration. Discernment turned out to be enlightening in knowing who was of like-mind and who wasn't. As I refined my choices, I learned to connect with people of similar vibration, the events became more fulfilling and impactful, and my life opened up in the same way. At the same time I blossomed in the communities that inspired me, so, too, did my personal relationships. Community was a place to practice creating my tribe.

I started taking short trips to Southern California and Lake Tahoe, where I could stay with friends or family. It was important to get my newfound sense of self out into the world. Reconnecting with my light helped open up my energy, such that I now have a business managing personal development events like those I had volunteered for in years past. By putting my energy into baby steps, it redirected me to where I wanted to go.

Please know, your dedication and belief is what make makes your path true for you too. You have within you the power to make your life what you want. Don't take rejection as an affirmation to hide your light because, sometimes, it takes three no's to make a "yes". Explore options and try others avenues. Even those that ultimately don't work out will show you there is more than one way to get where you're going. Have the confidence in yourself to keep going, recognize your strengths, and let go of any conditioning to the contrary.

Before I even knew about empowerment communities, I found ways to support myself with the tools I had. Whether you have a book for yourself or a best friend on speed-dial, create a touchstone to remind you of your inherent light. Choose tools and resources to connect you to your expansive self. Here are a few that I found to be extremely helpful:

- Practice gratitude for all that has been and will be.

- Meditate to surrender the noise of living and hear the hum of your inherent self.

- Surround yourself with people who resonate with positive life-force.

- Feel your connections with others to know that you're in the right place.

- Allow relationships to open you to growth experiences and amazing surprises you never thought your life would bring you.

- Be excited about possibilities.

The good and the bad, the light and the dark, all made me the woman I am today, and for that, I am grateful. I am also grateful for all that has made you into you. Remember that we create the life we live, so we can make it different. Choose your thoughts carefully, because your thoughts create your life. Expand your light into the world and find your tribe!

Biography

Jacquie Farquhar is a curator of inspirational events. She is passionate about creating environments that uplift people because she knows personal empowerment will change the world. Jacquie's JoyFULL Events, founded in 2009, is a business she has dedicated to producing events for motivational entrepreneurs who want to uplift and change the world.

It takes a person of unique character to elevate the art of caretaking into a business of coaching the coaches. In her years of service, Jacquie has developed a style of event planning that facilitates each of her clients stepping into their specialty, owning their voices, and focusing on being present to deliver their key messages while surrendering the intricacies of the venue, logistics, communications, and team management to her capable and loving hands.

Planning events for over twenty years, she learned the ropes of the hospitality industry early in her adult career and was soon coordinating events for 500+ people. Jacquie started her first business with $200 and within four years she grew it into a six figure business by applying her impeccable discernment, infinite resourcefulness, and innate rapport. She knows what needs to be done and leverages her adaptive and agile nature to resolve problems in the moment.

As a model of intuitive leadership, Jacquie builds trust among her team through clarity, collaboration, and contribution. She does not ask of others anything she would not be willing to do herself. Jacquie's key to team-building rests in creating an environment of respect, appreciation, and conviviality. It is important to her that her team walk away as fulfilled by the experience as the presenters and attendees.

Jacquie's natural gifts are implicit in the care she gives to every detail, every client, and every member of her team. It is truly a joy for Jacquie to see an event come together, and it gives her deep satisfaction to be a foundational role in her client's success. Jacquie's message to the world resonates clearly in her personal and professional life: "Each of us matters in our own unique way to make this world a better place for all."

Learn More...

jacqdt@gmail.com

https://www.facebook.com/groups/1116181778434130/

https://www.linkedin.com/in/jacquie-farquhar-18b75410

Section 4: Your Time Is Now!

In this action oriented, dynamic and inspiring section you will discover that your time is now! That there is an urgency to you stepping forward....to coming out of hiding and SHINNING! You will be inspired to share the gift of you with those around you. Heart by heart, and life by life. Tomorrow isn't guaranteed, we have today...now. If you are waiting for someone to give you permission to act now, please hear it in these chapters as they encourage you to take action NOW! Each chapter will cheer you and encourage you in the truth that NOW is your time. Not someday, but today. Enjoy this transformational set of chapters that will speak into your soul the truth that NOW IS YOUR TIME! Each author shares their story, truths, and powerful actions you can take to help you take action in your life now! We believe in you and can't wait to see you come out of hiding and SHINE!

Warmly,

Rebecca Hall Gruyter, Book Compiler and Empowerment Leader

How Defining Moments Led Me to Leadership
Linda Patten

When I woke up, my parents were not there. I was not in a private room at all. In fact, the beds all around me held little wizened children. I had awakened in a burn ward! I freaked out. I had been abandoned by my parents and sent to "hell." For what seemed a lifetime and was probably only about two hours, I laid there, afraid to look left or right, feeling totally abandoned before my parents finally found me to bring me to my room. This experience was so traumatic for me that for almost a year I did not talk and moved robotically through my days. Yes, I did finally come back to myself one night as my dad was watching me. He cried, and much later he told me they were not sure I would ever come out of the trauma.

This early, defining moment in my life stands out as paramount to my becoming who I am. Although over the years I learned how to build relationships and trust others, to this day I still have a fear of being abandoned by family, friends, and even clients.

A second life-defining moment may be better described as a series of moments in the form of a person. My grandmother's influence in my life was astounding. The words she spoke to me carried great weight. The soul deep beliefs from these words reverberated throughout all aspects of my life, from school to relationships to business.

Grandma was about 5'2" and 100 pounds soaking wet with a rod of steel in her back – a steel magnolia if there ever was one. She was not happy with the choice of a husband that my mother had made. A divorced Navy man who was five years younger than my mom was not someone my grandmother could love or respect. While I was too young to rationalize the relationship among these three people in my household, the impact on me was enormous.

Of course as a young person, I couldn't know how to describe what I now understand as tension in the house that you could cut with a knife. What I did know was that I could do nothing right in my grandmother's eyes and I was always accused of disrespecting her. I clearly became the target for my grandmother's frustrations.

One defining moment carved many quotes on my belief window. When I was seven, I took a drama class. It was so much fun and I was having a great time learning about speaking and being on stage. The program ended with a holiday performance, in which I was to memorize and present a poem. I had it down cold and I was ready. I got on stage; I spoke the words from my heart until the last two lines. I stumbled. My teacher was in the wings and gave me the first two words and I was back on track, soaring to the end of the poem. The audience stood and applauded. I was thrilled. I took my bows and left the stage triumphant. My family came backstage to see me, my mom and dad effusive with praise. However, my grandmother stood back. When I approached her she stepped back and said these fateful words: "It was okay, but you should never stand up in front of people and talk again." I was devastated.

For years, I was not able to talk in front of groups of people or lead them.

"Build high, strong walls around you, Dear…"

To add fuel to this fire, my parents, Grandma, and I (eleven years old) were on vacation. When we passed a group of kids my age, Grandma stopped them and said, "This is my granddaughter. You should play with her." Then she turned to me and said, "See, I have to make your friends for you. You just can't do it by yourself."

I was mortified, and after that, I never brought friends home because I was afraid of what she would say to them. My mother, perhaps an acorn not fallen far from the tree, would tell me to build high, strong walls around me as my "friends" would stab me in the back.

It has taken many experiences for me to exorcize the beliefs that my grandmother left with me. To this day, I have a few very close friends, and the thought still lingers sometimes in the back of my mind that they will hurt and abandon me. Even after being chosen many times to be the spokesperson or trainer, I was sure they had made a mistake and wanted someone else.

As a twenty-one-year-old 1st Lieutenant in the Army, I was selected from a large group of women at Fort Devens, MA to speak to high school students about joining the Army. I was later selected to train for the Women's Army Corps and appointed to the prestigious position of Protocol Officer for a 4-star General. Clearly the senior officers honored the leadership qualities they saw in me and were intent on mentoring me to become THAT leader. Once out of the Army, I went into the corporate world training and leading groups for Bank of America Southern California, North and South America, and Asia for the retail division of Crocker Bank and internationally for a training company. I spoke to more than 300 of my peers in the Convention Management arena.

With these successes, I finally believed that I could lead and effortlessly talk to groups of any size. However, I was still always the one behind the curtain who just made magic happen and hated to be publically recognized for it, deferring kudos to my team or client. I was very successful at hiding.

"I thought you would lead us..."

Sometimes in life there is that moment – that positive defining moment – when the right comment lands at the right time in the right way and changes everything. For me, it was a participant in a workshop who said to me, "I thought you would lead us in this exercise. It is what I expected of you." In that moment, I realized that all my life I had been meant to be a leader, to be in front of the curtain and to shine.

This wakeup call really had me look at the stories I was telling myself. It was true that I have been not only a talented trainer and an inspirational speaker, but also an exceptional leader. I had just never claimed it.

I couldn't know then what I know now. I needed to go through the wounding and the rebuilding to become the woman I am today. These old wounds helped me integrate the lessons I was to learn in this lifetime. They are a blessing, not a curse.

"You and your story matter. Step forward and shine!"

This statement is a foundation of my work with clients in my The Art of Herding Cats: Leading Teams of Leaders and Dare2Dream with Linda programs. Perhaps a fitting outcome of my own story is that I now help others uncover the natural leader inside themselves and I train leaders of leaders, particularly in the Network Marketing field. Many of these people are reluctant leaders and the story they tell themselves about leadership holds them back from shining as the extraordinary leaders they can be (and often already are but, like I was once, they're unconvinced that they are indeed leaders).

Is this something you can relate to?

To really step into your power, stand out, and shine requires you to change the stories that are keeping you hiding. What have you heard in your past that you continue to tell yourself now? You may have versions of the stories I've shared with you. Take some time to think about your stories and to assess if they really are true for you now. From that awareness, you can begin to take action in recrafting your life to a new story.

"Listen for the positive defining moments."

I am grateful for that defining moment – the positive one – when the workshop participant told me she saw me as a leader. I was open to hearing it and answering the wakeup call to look at myself differently. A new world opened up for me that continues to grow as I step out onto a bigger, global stage in my career. Listen for that moment, the one that can open your eyes to yourself and change the stories that keep you hiding. It can come from anywhere, unexpectedly. Don't miss it. It can change your life!

Another way to help you step forward and shine as a leader is to think about who has inspired you along the way. There may be surprising sources.

While my mom and I had a checkered past together, I now realize that it is my mom who really gave me the lessons that inspired my career choices as well as my values. I am glad I paid attention so I could appreciate and build on these lessons. My mom was a force to be reckoned with, and this is what she inspired me to do in my work and in my personal life:

- Be the person who has "control", the one making the decisions and determining the plan of action.

- ALWAYS have integrity. She was very clear that in whatever I did, it was never an acceptable choice to lie, cheat, or steal.

- Be strong as a woman and a leader. She was herself a leader in her community, her profession, her church, and as a mother. I saw her as someone who was firmly grounded in the present and yet had a clear vision of the future.

- Have a dream of how my life will be led, and follow it. When I look backward at what I have accomplished and the dreams that have been fulfilled and then forward to the dreams I have set for my future, I know that her advice and wisdom helped make me the success that I am.

The lessons I've learned and the mistakes I've made have led me to come out of hiding and shine. The "shine" part for me is that I can take away the pain to help move others into that place of power. My superpower is to step in and hold space so that others can create their vision and bring it into reality in that space. I am creating a new way for women to be successful through real transcendence - thriving, never to return to hiding.

My hope for you is that you look at the stories that have held you back, recraft your life with new stories, open yourself to the moments and inspiration that led you to change, and step into being the natural leader that you are – in your individual way, shining your special light.

Biography

Linda Patten is a leadership expert, event planner, entrepreneur, international speaker, and national bestselling author who shows women how to realize their ability to lead, to dream, and to create in their lives what inspires them. As someone who walks her talk, Linda is the founder and CEO of Dare2Dream with Linda and Wayneflete, Inc., both dynamic enterprises which express her passion to support women in business.

Through her programs and seminars, Linda takes her clients on a journey of self-discovery, personal empowerment, skill development, and a charted course toward becoming a leader of their own lives. At Wayneflete, she brings her forty years of experience in human resources, conference management, and event planning to free speakers and workshop leaders from the overwhelming burden of creating events, so that they can take the stage confidently and in their full brilliance. With this experience and fifteen years in network marketing, Linda is in a unique position to understand the art of herding cats, to teach you how to herd them too and to retain 20% more of your working consultants.

Linda holds an MBA in Organizational Behavior and Leadership, a Certificate in Meeting Management (CMM) as well as leadership positions in numerous professional management associations and women's business networking groups. She is the author of The Art of Herding Cats: Leading Teams of Leaders and guest contributor to Becoming Outrageously Successful: A Woman's Guide to Finding Her Purpose, Fueling Her Passion, and Unlocking Her Prosperity, by Dr. Anita M. Jackson. She speaks to audiences worldwide on topics of leadership and empowering women in business.

Visit her website, Dare2DreamwithLinda.com, or contact her at Linda@dare2dreamwithlinda.com.

Learn More...

linda@dare2dreamwithlinda.com

www.dare2dreamwithlinda.com

www.waynefleteinc.com

https://www.facebook.com/dare2dreamwithlinda

Fulfilling Your Life's Purpose
Jim T. Chong

"WHY?"

My hope in sharing my thoughts and life experiences is that they will inspire you to do something really big and to go after what you feel called to do in life...and to *NEVER GIVE UP!* As a professional Master Emcee, speaker, radio show personality, creator of The Wok Star, as well as a multi-cultural community leader serving actively on the executive team of several established organizations, I have been blessed with many opportunities to speak in front of hundreds and sometimes thousands of people at a time at events designed to advance cultures, communities, and commerce. I've chosen to help people in what I call the three M's: Money, Message, and Moments, which I will share about later. I like to help people break through the barriers that may be holding them back from doing something really big in life in helping others and creating their legacy.

By definition, if you want to affect the most possible amount of people in your lifetime, you must ensure that you can SHINE your light as bright as possible.

A wonderful friend and mentor, Kathy Fairbanks, shared a very insightful and valuable thought-provoking question recently with me that I needed to really think about. The question was "Why do I keep actively dimming my own light?" Immediately, my mind quickly started racing through the internal questions of "Am I really dimming my light?" and "I'm doing the best I can; what more can I really do?" However, when I allowed myself to reflect on the question, she was right and in actuality, I really did know the answer but I didn't want to admit it.

In many ways, I have been taught some great tools and have developed a strong belief system which has served me fairly well in life. What I realized, though, is that I can let my own "filters" affect how I interpret my own actions, which makes me second guess my own motives and therefore leads me to create my own self-sabotage. This is really hard to admit to myself. I think to myself, *Not me! I'm always working on doing the right thing and I am always giving...right?* True, but what I continually have to remind myself is that as I serve others, I need to ensure that I also create "wins" for myself along the way, or I will not be able to continue doing what I love to do. It's so easy to tell others to create a win for themselves, but it can be hard to implement personally. Ensuring we create win/win - or what I like to call "win for all" scenarios - is at times much easier said than done, especially for those that are cause-based. I find that cause-based people actually will create a win for others, yet often it will be at their own expense - or what we might know as a "lose" for themselves, which could be a form of self-sabotage.

In this way, we can hide from fully doing what we are called to do as a result of our own internal belief system. Then we are not creating a true win for ourselves and eventually we give up the life we are called to live. I must interject that sometimes we can be in hiding or in the shadows unintentionally and not even know it, even though we are publicly on the forefront of a cause.

I have often heard from others that are not financially stable but still about their cause, "I don't need to make a lot of money." Well, the question I often pose is, "If you had a million dollars, would having the money help you accomplish what you set out to do, making it more prolific and completed even more quickly?" Either that or we could be thinking, "It's not about me. I don't want to draw attention to myself and take away from the cause."

Well, speaking practically, if you don't focus on getting some level of attention and build your credibility, who is really apt to listen? These are questions that I had to personally wrestle with myself to ensure I could sustain my light shining brightly rather than eventually fading out. I am hoping that some of my life experiences and insights can help you increase your lumens and re-ignite your passion if it has been dimmed! Focusing on these questions will give you more passion to your purpose and help you design an even more powerful message. Money and Mindset are very important to achieving any goal and in helping you stay confident. Many people lose their confidence because one of these two things is faltering.

Do you overcome, or are you overcome during times of adversity?

What do you do when you face pain, a major obstacle, or challenge in life? One of the most iconic songs for me today is a song by Journey, "Don't Stop Believing". These three words are key to help keep us inspired and also hold the essence to not giving up on our dreams. The words remind us that we should not let go of our dreams, if we are ever to achieve them.

What were your dreams and aspirations growing up?

I didn't realize just how fast time would fly by. As we get older, time seems to accelerate. Yet every memorable event, when I spend some time in reflection, shaped me into who I am today. Understanding the precious moments in our lives help build our message to others.

Living for the PRESENT

If you are reading this, you have been blessed with yet another day, which should not be taken lightly. I am so excited about the wonderful opportunities that have been given to me in this lifetime. You remember the timeless famous phrase (which I will paraphrase) that states "The PAST is history, the FUTURE is what will happen, and the here and now is what we call the PRESENT, for it is a true GIFT. What will you do with your life...your PRESENT?"

Growing up...ah, yes, the time in life when things were so very simple and not complicated. Many of you are probably of my generation. We actually needed to be face to face with someone to actually talk with them - no smartphones, no Facebook, and we actually made time to have meaningful talks with each other over the table rather than stare at our phones.

As I grow older, I learn to appreciate the value of a moment. Time seems to be moving ever so quickly and I am understanding more just why we should make every moment count in our lives. Growing up, there were many life lessons that were experienced, whether through a victory or some obstacle that challenged us in some way. The key is to reflect and create value from them.

Lessons from Life

In looking back, I had to crack a smile reminiscing about how fortunate I have been. Mom always had food on the table and Dad worked hard on his job as a produce manager for the majority of his life. I had grown up in a somewhat simple setting in Marysville, California (Go Marysville High School INDIANS!). It was at a time when video games were the craze and friends got together and actually did things, where we had person-to-person interaction. Yes, going to a school dance was a big deal, and asking a girl we liked if they would like to dance was definitely a time of inner struggle and facing our fears...teenage style!

My mom only knew a bit of English and she spoke in what many today know as "Ch-english". I remember my dad coming home for lunch and resting on his favorite recliner before going back to work. My mom always had lunch and dinner ready and my dad always provided for the family. Thinking back, our house really couldn't have been much larger than a humble 1,000 square feet, although I never really gave it much thought back then.

My fondest memories were of getting together with friends and just doing things together, talking about girls and riding our bikes and getting from here to there. During my era, we enjoyed special historical events like the disco era, the release of the VCR, and the major milestone of music being captured on something called a CD as well as the release of *Star Wars* and *Rocky* on the big screen.

I was extremely fortunate to have enjoyed some very special moments in life which I reflect on and I must admit, I have taken them for granted. Going to U.C. Berkeley for college, I would experience new and different things.

Fortunately, I was always surrounded by people that had a sense of purpose in their life. Since the college days, various opportunities connected me closely with people that in many ways helped keep me sheltered from much pain and hardship. Growing older, I was blessed to have a beautiful wedding with the then-love of my life, which would lead to my two wonderful children, Jeremy and Sabrina. I had truly been blessed with many friends and opportunities, living the life that some only dream about. It wasn't until I received an unexpected call after midnight on October 9th, 2007 informing me that my mom had passed away that evening that life stopped for me and I had to really assess what was important in life. I had never experienced being informed directly of the death of someone I loved dearly, so this was a shock for many reasons. Following that, a devastating situation also directly happened to an immediate family member, which would reveal the weaknesses in my marriage, leading to a separation and an inevitable divorce.

One cannot truly understand but can only describe the pain of separation either by death or divorce. This was something I had only helped others with, not truly understanding the experience. Fortunately, I chose to keep myself busy rather than shutting down. However, it was a time of grave disappointment and true soul searching as to what was really most important in life. I did my best to have the talks and reflection time necessary to ensure that I would be dealing with the growing feelings of resentment, hate, and guilt, to name a few. Those moments helped me understand just how precious life really is.

Being in front of the room frequently, whether it be as a facilitator, speaker, or emcee, I have always enjoyed engaging with audiences and telling stories. I have chosen to engage people and not let the pain and obstacles get in the way. This is by no means an easy task, but I am grateful to have the friends and support to see me through the emotionally tough times...the moments that would build my message to others.

"Just Do It" - NIKE

Currently serving as a part time caregiver for Dad, whose memory is fading, I appreciate my life and every day I am blessed with. I understand that with every breath taken, it is a breath that could be used by someone else, so I am grateful and always look for value in life's lessons. As mentioned in the beginning, I choose to make my life count and help others deal with the three M's: their Money, Message, and Moments. MONEY drives every choice we are able to make, the MESSAGE helps us motivate and inspire others, and the MOMENTS in our lives give our message a solid foundation.

My hope is that you can go well beyond what you can dream or imagine and fulfill your purpose. As ELO sang about in the 70's, "Hold on tight to your dreams." Remember, success in life is defined by you. ***SUCCESS IS NOT ACHIEVED BY CHANCE, BUT BY CHOICE!*** Here's to your success. If you have a story, I would love to hear it.

Biography

Jim T. Chong is a Master Emcee and professional speaker, a licensed financial professional, and the founder of Solutions4Life and the Wok Star. He is a radio personality in the Greater Sacramento area on MONEY 1055FM as the Wok Star on "Rush Hour For Success". Jim loves to help people "SHINE" and is actively involved on the Executive Team of several established non-profit and cause-based communities and organizations in his local area. He excels in helping support those that wish to gain more influence and exposure in their local community by helping support them "SHINE" either as their Master Emcee or through social media. Jim supports and facilitates several workshops and programs such as the "Central Valley Recovery Awareness Preventing Strokes" (CV-RAPS) monthly program, which is at St. Joseph's Medical Center in San Joaquin County on behalf of Healings In Motion (http://www.healingsinmotion.org). He also provides bi-monthly inspiration, personal development, and character/leadership talks for the Central Valley Asian American Chamber Of Commerce IMC program and other organizations.

Jim is a sought-after emcee who consistently speaks in front of hundreds of people monthly. He has also emceed the Vietnamese Lunar Flower Festival in the city of Sacramento as well as the Chinese New Year's Parade and Festival in Stockton City with thousands in attendance. Jim has served as the Master Of Ceremonies to various established organizations and speaker venues. As of the time of this book being developed, he will be emceeing the Asian Festival in the town of Locke, California in May 2016 and had recently briefly appeared on the national program for the Travel Channel in *Ghost Adventures*. Jim has also helped produce award-winning short films and is a co-owner of In Motion Theatre Company along with Cami Ferry, which gives a portion of its profits back to a designated cause.

Through the "Wok Star" personality, Jim is passionate about advancing culture, community, and commerce by establishing collaborative venues and he is looking forward to the launch of his global radio show, "Live Strong America-Radio To Inspire", "CEO Leadership

Corner" with Jon Taber, as well as Wok Star Multimedia Publishing. Jim gets his fulfillment supporting the greater good by helping individuals' dreams come true by developing strategies for their money, message, and moments in life. Jim can be reached at jim@thewokstar.com or directly at (209)534-8000.

Learn More...

jim@TheWokStar.com

jtc.wokstar@gmail.com

http://www.TheWokStar.com

http://www.WokStarNation.com

Sometimes All a Girl Really Needs Is...
A Timeout and a Chance to Push the Reset Button
Nina Price

"There's something happening here... What it is ain't exactly clear..."
~ Buffalo Springfield

Last year I turned sixty and many of the things that happened to everyone else I know at an earlier age finally happened to me. My youngest daughter got married and left home: an empty nest. My oldest granddaughter turned eighteen and left home. My parents, too, turned a corner. Dad turned ninety and Mom turned eighty-seven. Each time I dutifully visited them, they seemed older and less able to manage things, yet more stubborn, determined to stay in their home and resist change. Finally they required in-home care, even though they were determined to resist it. It was hard to watch. In each case, I felt uneasy and sad.

There were other subtler things too. I moved my office to a new location, which turned into a bigger deal than I thought it would, not to mention the disastrous impact it had on my business. There were days when I never left the house because I just couldn't deal with the rest of the world. Nothing big or catastrophic happened. It was just a bunch of small losses, which added up to one big multifaceted loss, and I was feeling miserable. To cope, I went into escape mode. Without realizing it, I gave myself a timeout. I read more novels last year than I've read in my entire adult life. I was in hiding, and I was loving it.

The only thing I could do to cope was to check out. I was numb. I couldn't feel anything, and my brain couldn't seem to process things. Things that would be easy at other times, like making a simple decision, my brain couldn't be bothered with. I kept going through the motions: putting one foot in front of the other, seeing my clients, doing the laundry, eating crunchy pretzels, and reading and reading and reading. Escape into fiction was wonderful. I had forgotten how nice it felt to escape into a good story. I read Jane Austen fan fiction. Elizabeth Bennett and Fitzwilliam Darcy became my new BFFs. I read thrillers, whodunits, even young adult romance, fantasy, and although I can't believe I'm admitting this, even a couple of vampire romance series.

Vampire romances were more compelling than dealing with my life! Anything was more compelling than feeling the feelings of loss and despair that I couldn't bear to feel.

As I'm writing this six months later, looking back at it, last Fall my life was both ridiculous and pathetically funny at the same time. The good news is that when the New Year dawned a few months later, it was as if a switch flipped and I was magically back to myself. The switch flipped at New Year's because I made a decision last Fall, in the midst of hiding, to start making some changes. Even though there was something delicious about hiding, I knew I needed to get back to reality and a saner way of living life. Although I didn't realize it at the time, I can now see with the perspective of 20/20 hindsight that what I did for myself was exactly what I encourage my clients to do. Even though I was in hiding and not very functional, I nonetheless managed to "walk my talk" without realizing it.

I focused on three strategies that I've found to be essential to making the most of the midlife transition.

- *Divest Yourself of Old Baggage: Ditch What No Longer Serves You*

- *Prepare Your Body for the Long Haul: Become A Master of Self Care*

- *Push the Reset Button: Reinvent At Least One Aspect of Yourself*

Strategy #1: Ditch What No Longer Serves You

Ditch What No Longer Serves You is about ridding yourself of all the things in your life that no longer work for you. It's quite simply all about eliminating barriers to your success. Some years ago I learned to get rid of physical possessions on a regular basis, something I was not very good at, when a friend of mine challenged me to get rid of ten possessions a week. Every week for year I got rid of ten things: books, clothes, stuff in drawers, in cupboards, in my garage, in the trunk of my car – just ten things a week. Some weeks I even exceeded my quota!

Last fall, after my last child and her stuff left home, I realized that it was time for a "whole house purge". For three months I measured my success each week by how full my garbage cans were on trash night. I hired help to keep me on track and to help me with the tasks that were especially difficult for me.

The transformation after three months of house purge was phenomenal. We had cleared out so much stuff that the energy of the house changed dramatically. Clearing out the old stuff that no longer served me created space for new ideas, new clients, new learning, new practices, and new abundance to come in.

What helps you to get into action to do something you know you need to do, but lack the motivation to do?

There are other kinds of things you can ditch – like unproductive ways of dealing with people. What about intangibles? There are non-physical things that we need to ditch: relationships, beliefs, priorities, habits, activities, attitudes...

Have you ever "broken up" with a longtime friend because the relationship didn't work for you anymore? Do you have some relationships that aren't working for you anymore? If so, what do you want to do about them?

What areas in your life no longer work?

- how you spend your time

- who you spend your time with

- work/career

- your commute

- where you live

- your appearance – hair, skin, body

Once you're clear about what no longer serves you, how will you ditch or change these things? Check in with yourself to see if you need support or help with accountability.

Strategy #2: Become a Master of Self Care – Inside and Outside

As teenagers, our bodies change as our reproductive years begin. We need to learn how to deal with our new bodies and new responsibilities as we prepare for adulthood. In midlife, our bodies change again as our reproductive years end. Our brains and our attitudes change. We're no longer willing to put up with what we used to. We need to learn how to deal with our new bodies and new responsibilities as we prepare for the next stage of adulthood. Many of our ancestors never lived as long as we have. But we can expect to live 30, 40 or 50+ years past menopause! For this reason alone, how we navigate menopause is crucial to our quality of life going forward. If you consciously prepare yourself for your "next chapter", you can set yourself up for more energy, vitality and overall better quality of life as you get older. Self-care starts with self-awareness, becoming extremely aware of our bodies, and tuning in to what they're telling us, then giving our bodies what they need.

Many of us are so busy working and taking care of others that we're not paying attention to the messages our bodies are sending us. **Are you listening to what your body is telling you? Are you giving yourself enough "me time" to pay attention to yourself and your body? Are you taking healthy and nurturing actions?**

Hiding was my way of not feeling the feelings of sadness and loss last year. Being active and staying fit are especially important when you're feeling depressed. In Chinese medicine, when you're depressed, we say that your "qi is stagnating". The best way to get qi moving is to be active.

In my fifties I made the decision to become fit for the first time in my life. I hired a personal trainer and I started to work out regularly. Eight years later, I'm still at it. I'm more fit than I've ever been in my life. You're never too old to become fit and the benefits are significant. The more you take care of your body, the better it can take care of you.

Other areas that my clients and I have made changes in:

- Food – how, when, and what we eat

- Sleep – how much and when we sleep

- Sex – how we feel about sex after menopause, how we promote vaginal and intimate health

- Energy – how we cultivate energy so we can do all the things we want to

- Mental stamina – how we cultivate memory and brainpower

- Boundaries – how we create and enforce healthy boundaries to promote better relationships with others

- Our attitudes – how open we are to change and new ways of doing things

What messages is your body sending you?

What will you do to cultivate your body so that it will support you best?

Strategy #3: Reinvent at Least One Aspect of Yourself

I often talk about "turning an ocean liner" when I talk about change, and how a one-degree change can have a huge long-term impact. The same is true for you. One tiny "baby step" toward change is the beginning of what can be a bigger reinvention!

How many of you like to change your haircut every so often? Isn't that a reinvention of how you look? What is one thing that you want to invent or reinvent? When you view reinvention as a series of smaller changes, it doesn't seem overwhelming at all. Now's the time to come out of hiding, reinvent, and shine!

I reinvented my professional self completely during midlife. When I passed my licensing exam and got my acupuncture license my brother, who's an attorney, said that he admired the fact that I completely reinvented myself professionally. He said he wasn't sure he would have had the guts to do something like that. And honestly, I'm not suggesting that you have to do what I did. But I do think that reinvention during midlife is essential.

I say this because I see plenty of women who aren't reinventing themselves. They're doing what they've always done, looking the way they've always looked, being who they've always been, and it's stale, it's boring. I don't think they're very happy. But they're comfortable being stuck where they are. Remember: fear hates change, but success requires change.

My client Renee was really stuck and really depressed. She was very trying to be with and she was miserable. One day I quoted Albert Einstein to her: "Insanity is doing the same things over and over again, and expecting different results." I challenged Renee to change one thing in her life during the next month. I didn't care *what* she changed, just that she changed one thing in her life. Even though I wasn't specific about what I wanted her to change, she made the one change I hoped she would make – and it saved her life. She recovered from her depression and became a better version of her old self, and so can you.

By ditching what no longer served me, focusing on self-care, and reinventing aspects of myself, I, too, recovered from my depression and quit hiding. Because I devoted the Fall to working on improving myself, as the New Year dawned, I felt like myself again and I started working on some exciting new projects. I wish the same for you. "If you don't have a dream – how're you gonna have a dream come true?" (South Pacific) Start today. Clarify your dream and take the first step toward who you want to become. If I can be of service to you as you transform yourself, send me an email and let's set up some time to "tawk".

Biography

Nina Price is "The Queen of Midlife Transformation". She is, quite simply, Not Done Yet. With an M.B.A. from the University of Michigan, she is a former Silicon Valley high tech marketing exec who, after twenty years in the computer industry, learned that "it was time to do something else". In 2001, she pushed her own reset button and reinvented herself as a midlife success coach and board certified healthcare professional (a licensed acupuncturist and master herbalist) so she could solve more kinds of problems. She serves women tackling the transformations that come with midlife and beyond.

Nina lives in the Silicon Valley with her husband. She has two grown daughters and six grandchildren. For fun, she is a radio DJ who hosts a weekly music show and produces audiobooks for Audible.

Learn More...

ninapricelac@gmail.com

www.ninaprice.com

www.midlifewithoutcrisis.com

Meeting Destiny on the Road
Michael Anne Conley

"Destiny is like a stick in the middle of the road that you try to ignore, but you keep tripping over it until you have to pay attention."

~ Richard B. Miles

Author, holistic health pioneer

~~~~~

A memory unfolds. A snowball fight. I'm playing with the other kids. Reaching down, fast and furious. Duck! Toss! Whammmm!

All of a sudden Donna is crying and bloodied. Adults come rushing in. Looming over us, they blame me for hurting her — on purpose. No! No! We were just playing. I didn't know a rock was in the snowball!

But at nine, I'm reminded, I'm older than she is. I should have known to be more careful. Someone is at fault.

It will be me.

~~~~~

I grew up hearing, "You're the oldest. You should know better."

By the time I was nine, I already had eight years of experience with this. The message was mixed, containing a biological truth with a social expectation that was far from the truth. It's like a job with lots of responsibility, but no authority. I learned to feel incompetent, since the task was bigger than I could handle. I learned to hide my inadequacy, because it was unacceptable to be vulnerable. I learned to feel resentment about being put in this position.

This planted in me an attunement to injustice, which became a path for growth. How I found my way through this has been a profound and powerful journey.

A big lesson arrived one month to the day after my sixteenth birthday.

~~~~~

A memory unfolds. It's early on a Tuesday morning. Hours before the usual time, my father awakens me. In a serious voice, he tells me to get up.

Instantly, I feel angry. I know someone has died, probably my grandmother in California. Why wake me up for this, I think, dragging myself out of bed and following him down the hall. I bring my attitude into this scene: my mother sitting on their bed, surrounded by my siblings. Her head bowed in anguish, her hands gripping, she stares at nothing. His voice strained, my father says that our fifteen-year-old brother, Les, hospitalized for the last week, is dead.

The room erupts with sobs.

My own tears are complex. Guilt over my spitefulness mingles its tentacles into grief.

~~~~~

Having visited Les the night before, I was the last of us to see him alive. We were born a year apart, sharing fifteen years of friendly companionship. He died sixty-nine days before the first human heart transplant, which today would have given him life.

I kept the secret about my attitude for twenty-five years. I did not know it then, how this convergence of tragedy and awakening would become a formative event for guiding my life. But before I could fully appreciate this, I wandered in a desert of subterfuge.

Have you ever done something you felt ashamed about, but didn't want to face?

At first, I couldn't handle the awakening part, that snippet of awareness about my misplaced resentment. So I kept my secret hidden, pushing the memory away. The year following Les's death provided plenty of distraction. It was 1968 and cracks in the nation were widening with assassinations, anti-war dissent, and riots. Isolating myself in my bedroom, I numbed my personal pain by focusing on that contentious election. I'd already been a high school journalist, and newspapers seemed to be uncovering injustice and telling truth. Within two years, I had found a career.

It was an adventure. For a decade, I pursued making a difference with passion and direction. But destiny started tripping up these plans for professional success, pointing me instead toward personal healing. A single decision to support a friend in a thirty-day diet meant abstaining from my daily Dr. Pepper habit. Surprise! The incessant gnawing in my gut disappeared. Then, surprise again! It flared right back up as soon as I ended the diet. This link between what I ate and how I felt physically was compelling.

It was also getting harder to hide my unhappiness. Discovering the human potential movement led me to make connections between what I had buried about myself and how I felt emotionally. Also, I began to realize my values did not fit with the media's interest in the status quo and celebrity. My passion for mainstream journalism was waning. In the 1970s, there was no Internet, no ready path for publishing my own voice, so my explorations in health and personal growth offered another way to learn and share truth.

Although I was still a stranger to an interior life, seeds had been sown.

~~~~~

"When we meet real tragedy in life, we can react in two ways: either by losing hope and falling into self-destructive habits, or by using the challenge to find our inner strength."

~ His Holiness, the 14th Dalai Lama

~~~~~

My self-destructive habits with food, alcohol, drugs, and relationships actually helped me find inner strength. After years of hiding, possibilities began to show up. In graduate school, one significant experience gave me an opportunity to grow through darkness and shine.

~~~~~

A memory unfolds. This time, I'm on the receiving end of someone else's experience of injustice.

"Who do you think you are?" one woman says.

Another pipes up, "You're not an alcoholic. What do you know?"

"Your parents weren't drug addicts," says a third. "How dare you!"

I'm at the alcoholism treatment center where I'm a new student counselor, facing more than a dozen unfriendly women. Not knowing what else to do, my supervisor has told me she's giving them their say.

One at a time, they spit their rage. It goes on and on without interruption, and there's no permission for me to respond. This is not a search for understanding. I feel devastated and mystified by their words and betrayed by my supervisor's silence.

I know that I can walk away from this internship, but it's too important to discover what's really going on, and how I participated in it. So I decide to return — and learn.

~~~~~

The women's feedback had no ring of truth on the surface, so understanding my role took patience. Fortunately, my graduate school expected students to attend to our own healing as an essential part of our new careers as health professionals. This fit my values. My learning curve was steep and hard, this incident being one among many.

Along with my interest in holistic paths to health, by the time I walked into that recovery center I had already stepped away from alcohol and drugs as solutions for myself. I had started understanding family dynamics, reinforced by my own experiences, including my brother's death. Also, I had just begun to learn a new way to dive into myself, a body-centered practice that went deeper than diet and fitness models. It gave me practical ways to find peace of mind that I had never successfully experienced through meditation.

My time with the women led me further into this experiential process. I began to recognize how I had absorbed the expectation that I should know better. I had made this belief my own, pressuring myself with the *demand to know*, especially when I felt inadequate. With my therapist's support and the body-centered framework of my mentor, I began learning to take charge of my reactions — within myself, as well as toward others.

This practice was a master key that helped me begin to unlock questions about self-pressuring and inadequacy, about resentment and injustice, and so much more.

~~~~~

"Insight can be important, but to know is not enough. To alter your life situation is to be able to change your function. This is not merely to change your mind, but to change the way you use yourself."

~ Stanley Keleman, *Somatic Reality*

~~~~~

In that dark experience, I could have hidden from myself yet again. Instead, by choosing to enter myself with intention, I was able to create small flickers of light that moved me toward managing my emotional states. In that situation, learning how to use myself was a gift — of knowing how to survive the heat of someone else's blame and not fall into my own. What a relief it was to have something I could do for myself whenever I wanted!

I also discovered a new sense of direction. It was important to do more than just teach *about* holistic health. Just as I had been supported in learning and living my own truths with more satisfaction, I wanted to support others in finding their own hope and solutions.

In this exploration, a template emerged that I developed over time, and still use when challenging experiences call for compassionate self-care. I've shared this in my thirty-two years of helping others deal with their own struggles, so here it is for you:

The 2% Feedback Solution

- Be empathically curious. Knowing your own truth from felt experience, without dismissing the truths of others, connects your head with your heart.

- Walk in the question. This is not a time for figuring things out, but one of inquiry. Allow answers to arrive in their own way. Each turning point has its own timing, and it will patiently wait to unfold its messages.

- Seek the 2% that's true. What others say and do is inside them. Even when their feedback doesn't seem to fit, reach beneath your surface. Actively and humbly search for what *might* be true about you, even if it means making friends with what you've hidden from yourself.

- Incubate. Steep yourself in mystery and be not afraid. Your unknowns, no matter how dark they feel, need not bury you. New wisdom is waiting to come to light.

- Get support. Don't let your feelings, or your fear of being seen, prevent you from seeking guidance. To isolate is an injustice against yourself.

~~~~~

"When we numb the dark, we also numb the light."

~ Brene Brown, *Rising Strong*

~~~~~

A memory unfolds. It is the weekend Les would have turned forty. I am sitting on a couch with three of my five siblings. They were ten, eight, and two when he died almost twenty-five years ago. I have spent months laboring over a letter that started as a journal entry to myself. Now it is time to tell my secret to them, and then to the rest of my family as well.

It's not just about the attitude I had when our father awakened me — but also about how my shame around it led me to separate myself from them. It's about how Les's death propelled me into each of the professions I have entered, another of my secrets. It's also about my awareness that we have been keeping our feelings about his death secret from each other. This room also flows with tears. This time, connection happens. Risking rejection, I have been blessed by understanding.

~~~~~

Formative experiences give shape to our lives. You can turn away from their lessons, just as I did for many years. Chances are, they'll be like the stick in the road that won't be ignored.

If you ever feel challenged by this, you'll find great resources on my website, www.habitsintohealth.com. You can also reach out for a more personal, private conversation. I support you in claiming your freedom from habits that hold you back from the future you want.

You deserve the peace of mind you'll experience when you take charge of these patterns instead letting them continue to rule you! There is real power in building skills for using yourself wisely, no matter what.

May your turning points include gifts of calm in the midst of pressure, from a deep place of self-knowing that sustains your life. I honor this in you as your birthright.

"There is a crack, a crack in everything. That's how the light gets in."

~ Leonard Cohen, Anthem

Biography

Michael Anne Conley, M.A., LMFT, is a private consultant who has been passionate about health and habit change for almost forty years. As a marriage and family therapist, she supports women who struggle with self-defeating habits that hold them back in their personal and professional lives.

As a young adult, Michael Anne was a journalist, including freelance work for *People* magazine and *The New York Times*. Faced with health issues, she began her healing journey and her transition from mainstream journalism into holistic health care in 1977. Michael Anne now has a thirty-two-year track record of bringing clients to a place of empowerment in the world of addiction recovery. Drawing on her professional expertise and leading by example from her own life, she created her Habits Into Health system to make this transformation possible for women in everyday life.

In addition to consulting, Michael Anne is a motivational speaker and leader of personal development programs. She continues to write, for example, offering readers access to practical and fulfilling possibilities through her book, *Do YOU HAVE a habit - or does your habit HAVE YOU? 5 warning signs that you're stuck and what to do about it.*

Michael Anne holds a master's degree in clinical holistic health education and is the founder and director of Stillpoint integrative health center in Lafayette, California, USA.

Michael Anne says, "I am passionate about helping women take their next steps because I believe that when women become change agents in their own lives, they transform the world."

Learn More...

info@habitsintohealth.com

http://www.habitsintohealth.com/breakthrough-consultation/

http://facebook.com/habits.into.health

https://www.linkedin.com/in/MichaelAnneConley

Rediscover Your Wings and Soar
Phyllis Flemings

You are important by being yourself. As Marianne Williamson stated in her bestselling book *A Return to Love: Reflections on the Principles of a Course in Miracles*, "You are powerful beyond measure." You can be, do, and have everything you desire. You can design your life. It is never too late to realize and live your dreams. You can make the contribution to the world you are here to make.

Women, no matter what their age, have a tremendous amount of wisdom to offer. By the time you reach 50, 60, or 70, you have a wealth of knowledge to share with the world. Never is there a better time than now to believe in yourself. Never is there a better time to live your life with passion and be the person you were created to be. Women no longer have to accept less pay because of their gender.

I have always been one of those women who did more than what was expected, careful to not draw attention and judgment or outshine anyone else. Out in the workforce, I ended up getting promoted very fast. In my quiet way, I was successful because you cannot hide the light our Creator has instilled in you. Fresh out of college, I was among 250 applicants chosen out of 2,000 to be part of the Carter Administration's Presidential Management Intern Program. Later, I had the distinction of being the first woman to hold a significant management position (in my particular field) in an organization that had been in existence for over thirty years. My supervisor had insight and felt that I was the best candidate for the position.

When I was born, my mother already had three children and they were out of the house. She did not expect to have more children. My father died when I was two years old. My mother told me that God knew that He was taking my dad, so God sent me. Telling me that story made me feel good about myself. Growing up, summers and Christmas breaks were spent in Chicago, but my mother and I lived in the South the rest of the year. I really felt like I had four parents because my older siblings treated me as if I was their child, as they had no children at that time.

My mother raised me to be independent. It was not a matter of if I was going to college, it was where I'd go. Education was very important to my entire family and I benefited from their generosity to attend college. I was even able to study a number of years in Spain and I discovered my passion to make a difference in the world during my time abroad. I have an undergraduate degree in Government & Politics and a Master's in Public Administration. I later received a Ph.D. in Spiritual Coaching.

I participated in my church even at a young age: singing, teaching, speaking, and doing what I enjoyed. As a young child, I was very smart, involved, and active. When I went to school, the teachers saw my talents and used me in plays as leads and I was given many opportunities to shine. It felt natural to be doing what my Creator had designed me for.

However, even though adults and younger children appreciated what I did, my peers did not. I would hear things such as "who do you think you are?" and "you are not all of that." It didn't take too long for me to not want to volunteer and I started to put myself in the background because I wanted others to shine. I thought that was the right thing to do.

Despite my attempts to live in the shadows, I was able to move up and succeed in many areas and in my own quiet way, make a difference. I felt, though, that I had to do so much more to prove to myself that I was deserving and okay. Pleasing others was very important to me and I've done that for years, even to the point of putting myself in jeopardy.

Playing it small to keep others from feeling intimidated or feeling "less than" has not served me at all. Not wanting to be judged or not wanting to hurt others has kept me from being all that I can be. Keeping myself on the path of coming out of hiding includes sharing my brilliance.

For a long time I felt that I had to do more and I had to learn more...because being me wasn't enough. I have multiple coaching certifications and could paper the walls with other program certifications. In the end, I've learned that no one can tell you who you are or what you can or cannot do.

You must go within to get the answers. You can live your life with passion and be the person you were created to be.

I see the hero in people. I support each person in seeing that Spirit so that he or she can see who he or she is meant to be and have the impact they are supposed to have on the world. All my life I have known that there was something I was here to share and I know that I am here to help people rediscover their wings and soar. I am here to support them in making the contribution that they are here to make. I help them to see that there really is no failure. There are only lessons that we learn on the way to help us grow and become more of who we really are.

I am coming out of hiding to share my gifts with love and gratitude in a more powerful way. My gifts are to train, coach, and lead others to become their passionate self and to offer their gifts to the world.

If I could go back in time and impart the wisdom of my present self to my younger self, I would say this: *Be yourself, for there is no other person on the planet who is just like you. You have a lot to offer, and hiding your light does a disservice to the world and to you. You are a loving, kind, and compassionate being. Listening to naysayers is never a good idea. You have the power now. Listen to that small inner voice and do not allow others to take away your dreams.*

Know that you are here for a reason and connect with your passion and live your passions. Love God, yourself, and others. Be grateful for all things. Remember that nothing is bad. Everything that happens in your life can be used as a lesson to help you move forward and grow. Believe that you deserve good. You have right now everything you need to be, do, and have all that you desire.

Your path is your path, meant only for you. Everybody's path is not the same. Don't judge another's path and don't let another move you from what you believe.

When I was a little girl, I had dreams about being an actress. I loved going to the movies and being swept up in all the stories. One day, my sister got tired of me talking about being an actress and asked me to look at the actresses. She pointed out that none of the actresses I admired looked like me. The ones who were in the movies and looked like me had parts that I didn't want to play as maids or even less glamorous roles. I let that dream go. I didn't see color when I had watched the movies on the screen, or even when I'd been on stages in school. I loved putting on another character. She pointed out that the outside world had a different perspective.

I may have gotten older, but I still have my perspective and I have made the choice that the world is friendly and a good place.

I believed that if I asked for something, because I was loved, things would happen. I am grateful for everything. I'm grateful because of what I've learned. I've learned lessons from everything that has happened in my life. In the long run, it's for my good and my growth when I look at it that way. I have learned to be more cautious and conscious in my life. I still take risks and trust that I am moving in the right direction.

Today, I am rediscovering my wings and I am soaring. I'm coming out boldly and letting people know what I do and giving them an opportunity to work with me. I support women who are interested in living a passionate life and making the difference they are here to make. I am a great seminar/workshop leader, a transformational speaker, and a supportive and nonjudgmental coach who will stand beside you at all times.

I have always had the companionship of my Creator, my Source, and now with that partnership, I will move into my greatness. My purpose is to work with others to be who they were created to be, to help them find their passions and move into their purpose.

As Janet Attwood stated in the New York Times bestseller *The Passion Test,* by Janet and Chris Attwood, "When you are clear, what you want will show up in your life and only to the extent that you are clear." I am on a mission to support others to know their passion and purpose. I am clear and know that as I allow myself to be lifted up and come out of hiding and shine, I can do the same for you.

I would like everyone to have the opportunity to be clear about his or her purpose in life. Please go to www.phyllisflemings.com to receive "Top Five Reasons to Know Your Passions". When you are aligned with your deepest, most important passions, the ups and downs of daily life won't be able to throw you off track.

You are a blessing. You are important by being yourself. Remind yourself with daily affirmations that:

I can be, do, and have what I desire.

Everything I need is within me.

I can design my life.

It is never too late to realize and live my dreams.

I can make the contribution to the world I am here to make.

My time is now to show up and shine!

Spread your wings and soar!

Biography

Phyllis Flemings, PhD, is the founder/owner of Phoenix Rising Again, where she supports women in rediscovering their wings so that they can soar and live a passionate life. She is a Certified Life and Success Coach, a Law of Attraction Coach, a Know Your Why Coach, a Certified Passion Test Facilitator, a trainer, and speaker. Most of all, she is a student and a teacher who believes that we all are heroes who can be, do, and have what we want and that it is never too late to live our dreams.

Phyllis has been supporting people for over thirty years, helping them to see who they really are so that they can make the contribution that they are here to make. Because she believes that we already have everything we need in order to live the life that we desire, she is patient in taking the time necessary for others to see this for themselves. She is confident that we all have something to offer and can make a difference in our own lives as well as the lives of others.

Phyllis is always available for the client and her time is spent being open, non-judgmental, compassionate, kind, and present. She does not lose sight of her goal, which is to support the person in getting their needs met in a way that empowers them. She understands the process of going from here to there because she has her own experiences of overcoming as well as witnessing the experiences of others.

Learn More...

phoenixrising197@gmail.com

www.facebook.com/Phoenix-Rising-Again-106395113064552/

Simple Sparks
Katherine Johnson

There are many ways to hide in life. When I was hiding in plain sight, I used my clothes and appearance in two ways: as an invisibility cloak and as armor. I unknowingly cloaked myself and hid behind a wardrobe of clothes unconsciously perfected to blend in and protect me. For over a decade, everything about the way I lived and looked said, "Don't see me." I was a chameleon, adept at reading any situation and understanding how I needed to show up to meet someone else's expectations. The downside of this pretzel act was that I got farther and farther away from myself. I was training myself to look externally rather than internally for guidance on who I was supposed to be.

"Nobody even knows who you are."

These six words shook me. In a flash, they tore an opening that allowed me to wake up, explore a new way of seeing myself, and start showing up in my life connected to my true self. These six words were a gift from someone innocent, compassionate, and loving: my six-year-old daughter. And they were absolutely true.

I was sitting with my daughter at the playground after school. She was next to me nibbling on pretzels while her little brother played on the slide. I had been divorced for a few years and was still navigating what this next chapter of my life would look like. I had signed up for my very first personal development workshop, "Being On Purpose", and I told Riley that a babysitter was coming over that night so I could attend. Without skipping a beat, still looking out at the kids playing on swings, she said, "Why do they even want you there? Nobody even knows who you are." With those words hanging in the air, she skipped off to the monkey bars.

I could hardly process what she just said to me. I furiously thought to myself, "That is not true! Of course people know who I am. I have a degree from Princeton...I am important...I was a national-champion athlete." I was indignant and simultaneously nodding at how tired and expired those identities felt. That was the moment I realized something was wrong.

During that weekend's workshop I ripped open that crack and discovered that I had been hiding in plain sight. Nobody knew me because I didn't want to be seen. It is a strange day indeed when you realize that somewhere along the way, you've fallen asleep on yourself and become invisible. Did something happen that made me want to hide? Or was this something I did to myself, slowly, over time?

When I was growing up, I believed that my achievements were the only way to get recognition in my family. If I didn't try my best and win, I was a failure. It showed up in my way of being, as an athlete, and in the expectations I created for myself. By the time I was twenty-one, I had graduated from Princeton University, competed abroad multiple times representing the U.S. in international squash competitions, was the number one college squash player in the country, and had been named Player of the Year in squash by the US Olympic Committee. Following this trajectory, I looked out at the life ahead of me and anticipated an accomplished life living and working abroad, dynamic and unique experiences in life and love, and being one of the last of my friends to settle down and get married.

Less than two years later, my mom called early on a Sunday morning, telling me to come home. After many years battling cancer, my dad's health had suddenly taken the final turn and he was transitioning into hospice care. She told me to be prepared that he might not be alive by the time my plane landed. I arrived in time to sit with him and hold his hand for the last time before he died that night. I was only twenty-three years old. I was not prepared for how completely I would collapse. I was not prepared for the years of grieving and uncertainty I felt about who I really was. It felt like he took all the air with him when he left. Losing my father ignited an unraveling in me in which I shrank smaller and smaller, moving away from living my full potential. Somewhere deep inside, I unconsciously abdicated my responsibility to myself in exchange for safe harbor in a life that would take care of me. Within three years I was married, getting a master's degree, and seemingly content. Over the next ten years, I disappeared behind the expectation of how life was supposed to look: keeping busy with the perfect-looking marriage, raising a family, always looking forward. It was busy and looked normal, but I didn't feel normal. Looking inward, I felt inadequate, imperfect, and like an impostor. I was like a ghost living on the periphery of my own life.

"Knowing others is intelligence. Knowing yourself is true wisdom."

- Lao-Tzu, 6th Century Taoism

Going through a divorce is a grueling marathon, not a sprint. When my marriage ended after a decade, I was leaving the life I thought would be forever. It just wasn't the right life for me. I was in pain, terrified, and riddled with guilt. I was turning my family's life upside down and forcing a new reality upon my husband, my children, and all the extended family it affected. This was my first act of unconditional love towards myself, and it was unfamiliar and full of uncertainty. But I did it.

The first year living on my own, the early mornings were when the fear was overwhelming. I would awake at 4 a.m. with "the tightness" — a nauseous pit in my stomach, barely able to breathe, and terrified that I could not do this. I might fail my children and myself. Here I was an Ivy League graduate, an accomplished athlete, a successful professional — accomplishments that I thought would create feelings of confidence and competence — and I was crippled by fear. It was fear that I had chosen an impossible path, fear that I would fail as a mother, fear that I would forever struggle financially. Early morning mind chatter filled up my whole body, making it impossible to go back to sleep. I would cry in a fetal position until I heard the kids wake up, and then I would pull myself out of bed to be Mom again and get everyone ready for school.

So what changed for me? What changed in me?

One of the earliest steps in choosing myself as a priority was finding a place to live. The idea of living alone in a home frightened me. Would I be scared to be in the house alone when the kids were at their dad's house? How could I take care of a whole house by myself when I was still learning how to take care of myself? I preferred the idea of living in a bustling apartment building where I wouldn't feel alone. I was listening to myself and honoring what I heard, so I waited. We lived in an apartment that worked for us. Within six months, I felt more confident and eager to find a home for this next chapter of my life. On the first day of looking at homes, I made an offer on a one hundred-year-old bungalow that held lots of potential and felt right to me. Over the next six months, I would take the house down to the studs and look through the wood and nails to the basement below to see how the electricity and plumbing was routed through the walls. It was straightforward and uncomplicated. As the house was put back together with sheetrock, new fixtures, and finishings, I knew the house inside out. I was no longer afraid.

When my marriage ended, at first I struggled to find the thread that would connect me to my true self. Like many of the women I meet, by the time I hit forty, I had tried on a wide array of personas and had lived through several life chapters. In fact, I juggled so many different identities that I lost track of who I was supposed to be and for whom. I spent a crazy amount of time stuck in a chapter in which I micromanaged who saw which pieces of all the identities I artfully balanced - professional, friend, lover, mother, sibling, athlete, teacher, creative, partner, daughter. How could I possibly blame people for not knowing or respecting the real me?

What does it mean to feel seen, heard, and valued for who you truly are? When I think about the relationships in which I feel seen, people are seeing, enjoying, and embracing those parts of myself that I love the most: my sense of humor and enthusiasm, my compassion, and my ability to authentically connect with people. I didn't always feel safe sharing those parts of myself, even within my own family, and so I shared those parts discerningly. When I committed to unconditional love, I committed to being all of myself all of the time. What I have experienced is that this change in me radically changed the people who came into my life. My life now is full of compassionate, introspective, funny, creative, and inspiring people. By living as my true self, these people have been able to see me. The biggest change I made was to embrace myself.

What we communicate to ourselves impacts how we connect with others. All my energy is now positively focused on helping women come alive. Through my work, I teach women who want to be seen, heard, and valued for who they truly are how to dress authentically and confidently in the colors, fabrics, textures, and design lines that create resonance. I marvel at the women I meet through my work. They are full of life experience, compassionate, self-aware, complex, and eager to make a bigger impact in their lives. I teach them how to see themselves first and be intentional about framing themselves in the clothes and colors that are in harmony with who they are. Supporting women in this way is like blowing on an ember, creating a spark that ignites something bigger inside them so they come alive and commit to their own greatness. **It is never too late to show up in your life, get connected to your true self, and be confident in who you are.**

My phone rang not too long ago. It was a prospective client and within minutes of talking, the woman deepened our conversation with her honesty. "I look put together and I am successful on many counts, I frequently speak on stage to hundreds of people...AND, the truth is, I know I am hiding. I don't want to live this way anymore. I just want to be myself. It's important to me."

The thing about hiding in plain sight is this: nobody knows you are hiding except you. When you have an inkling that you might be stuck, that you want to be more for yourself, that nobody really knows you, there is an opportunity to see yourself in a different way, to shed the layers that are incongruent, and to show up more connected to your true self.

I invite you to explore a new way of seeing yourself, to connect with your true self and to be confident in who you are in this moment. Living as your true self starts with a commitment to unconditional love for yourself. Is it always easy? No. Is it scary? Sometimes. Does the commitment to unconditional love ever end? Not a chance. Is it worth it? Hell yes!

Biography

Katherine Johnson believes meaningful connections happen when we show up as our best selves. Before we even speak, our presence can help us connect or disrupt connection from happening. The psychology of first impressions, relationship building, and leadership highlights the importance of aligning what we are saying and who we are being. She teaches women how to gracefully amplify their presence and make a bigger impact in all areas of their life. An engaging international speaker and workshop leader, she spreads her message to help leaders, speakers, and professionals all over North America know the power of a seamless presence that communicates that they are comfortable, confident, and fully embracing who they truly are.

Katherine's proven model for aligning your presence from the inside out reconnects you with your core self, all the while helping you reclaim clarity, confidence, and courage to shine your light in the world. Whether it is knowing what to wear professionally, in front of a camera, or in your day-to-day life, Katherine revolutionizes everything you thought you knew about presence and personal style so you can connect more easily with others and position yourself for success. Through speaking, workshops, and transformative one-on-one work, Katherine supports women who want to be seen, heard, and valued for who they truly are. Her goal is to help women discover their authentic spark so they can feel more confident, experience joy living as their best self, and make a bigger impact in the world.

Even with an Ivy League education, high visibility as a national champion athlete, and success in the professional world, Katherine struggled to be authentically seen and live the impactful life she desired. This situation inspired Katherine to redefine what it means to live a purposeful life and create a business based on the truth of who she is and her core values. In this moment, her business spark was born. Instead of focusing on the clothes first, she is passionate about focusing on the woman and framing her in the clothes that create a memorable and congruent presence.

Katherine lives in Portland, Oregon and can be found having silly dance parties with her children, laughing with close friends, enjoying family camping trips, or running around the squash court. She loves traveling far and near to meet extraordinary women who are hidden treasures ready to shine their light in the world.

Learn More...

kj@katherine-johnson.com

www.katherine-johnson.com

www.facebook.com/sparkyoursignaturestyle

www.linkedin.com/in/katherinejohnsonpdx

Section 5: The Choice is Yours; Choose to SHINE!

In this powerful section you will hear stories of amazing experts that will encourage, empower and remind you that you get to choose. It is a choice to SHINE! Enjoy this motivational set of chapters that will speak into your heart and spirit that the choice is yours and we hope you choose to SHINE! Each author shares their story, truths, and powerful choices you can make! We believe in you and can't wait to see you come out of hiding and SHINE!

Warmly,

Rebecca Hall Gruyter, Book Compiler and Empowerment Leader

Home Is...
Brandy T. Jones

As a child in a military family, getting to know people in a new town always started with the same question: "Where you from?" I learned early on that even the simplest questions can have complicated answers. I began to tell people, "I know where I was born, but I'm from all over, because I never lived in one place long enough to call it home."

Not having any roots in my life has had far-reaching effects on me, my relationships, and how I interact with the world. It has also helped me grow and encouraged me to create consistency and constancy, even though it goes against all my conditioning.

I was always starting over, never really feeling settled or comfortable. I consistently felt out of place. Friendships were left behind when my family uprooted every four years or so. It was my job to do the packing and unpacking of the household. It was an assignment I volunteered for. I just knew it was something I could do for the whole family. It made me feel like I had a place of my own, even thought my surroundings were changing again.

What started as a disconnection from the towns I lived in spread through our family tree until I was a stranger from my extended family too. They only saw us between moves, which caused them to treat us differently. They acted like we thought we were better, because all they saw was us breezing into town before moving on to another exotic (or not so exotic) place. Even time spent with my grandparents was strained. Instead of a continuum of their loving care, our relationship was always stopping and starting.

This teeter-totter rhythm of my early life caused a real sense of motion sickness that had no pill for a cure. It was just one more way to make me feel off-balance. To this day, I start and stop projects because that behavior was conditioned in me from early on. I don't use that as an excuse, but it is a reason. We all have our reasons, and whatever they may be, they are not a free ticket to complain about life. Rather, we should use those reasons to accept what has happened and propel us forward.

Regardless of my private vertigo, my public face was set. Not fitting in was my little secret. I hid the truth from my parents, my brother, and my teachers at school. I was so adept at keeping this secret that at times I believed it myself. I became so proficient at adapting to new environments that it became a source of pride. I held myself to high standards in the classroom and in my relationships.

In military schools, we kids kept our heads down and connected with each other the best we could, knowing that any of us could be gone the next day. I entered civilian school in the seventh grade, but the same codes of conduct came with me. The girls on the playground assumed my carriage was a statement of acting better than the local kids and they threatened to take me down a notch or two. My secret was ultimately revealed when I came home from school in the beautiful dress my mother had made me, now dirty and torn from a fight to protect my honor.

The recurring fights just taught me to keep the feelings in my heart an even bigger secret. If I hid deep enough inside myself, I thought I would be protected. What was the point of having to repeat myself to the next new group of people when I'd be leaving soon enough?

Opening a door to my inner self would leave me vulnerable to the subject of gossip behind my back after I had moved on. It bothered me, even though I wasn't there, because I had an image of how I wanted to be perceived, and I was afraid of where those perceptions could go.

The irony of growing up on the road is that I was also able to mature in ways I would not have imagined. I learned about different cultures, peoples, and ways of living that I never would have been exposed to had I stayed in Florida. As a child, it was fun and rewarding to travel the world and meet new people. I did more in my first sixteen years than I ever would have by living in one place. The fact that I hid inside myself as a consequence seems bittersweet.

Maturing early in some ways made me feel like a naïve adult in others. I still want to belong to communities I live in, but don't necessarily feel connected with. To this day, I have the "new kid" feeling when I walk into a party and nobody knows my name (even if have lived in a neighborhood for years). I still worry about being judged before people get to know me first. I don't get in physical altercations anymore, but there is a part of me that wonders if there won't be a verbal disagreement because I don't fit into a box of someone else's making.

It doesn't serve me, trying to fit into someone else's idea of who I should be. I know to say no to that way of controlling me and a relationship. After a lifetime of not fitting in with the people around me, I learned instead to search for outsiders like myself and other travelers outside the box of "BFF's" (Best Friends Forever).

Then again, I didn't trust those relationships that maintained a status quo. I started to see a divide within, but I couldn't close the gap that got larger and larger as I became an adult. I finally realized what was missing. Connection. Family. Roots.

I thought because I was missing my roots, I had nothing to rely on, nowhere to go back to, no foundation to call my own. As a child, my connections were tenuous and nothing was concrete. My spirit wasn't settled. I didn't give people a chance to get to know me. I believed my childhood history and my adult legacy weren't connected. I was wrong.

Reflecting on my experiences prompted me to share with others because growing up in a family that moved all the time also had its rewards. Being the new kid in school also meant I understood at a young age what it means to have "beginner's mind." Feeling different meant I practiced what I later came to call "acceptance." I gathered up all my experiences, good and bad, to enrich my life by bringing them forward, out of the darkness and into the light.

In the past, I had allowed family circumstances to stop me. Before starting college, I knew I wanted to be a professional woman and have my own business. My mother told me I had to be a wife and make babies. I carried around regrets for years because I did not go back to get an Associate Degree until my daughter was out of college. By then, my work experience negated the need for further degrees. Still, I felt shame for not having the same kind of intellectual training as those I worked with at the university. I hid my shame with thoughts like, "I could've done that too, if only..." Then I tried hiding my true worth to avoid competition altogether. Because I had been the recipient of jealousy in the past, I dashed my own hopes before someone else beat me to the punch.

It took me decades to figure out my own shining truth about belonging. I am forever adjusting to belonging in the communities I travel through. I do things I've dreamt of doing all my life, and in so doing, I can allow myself to shine. I set my own rules. I do what makes me happy. I choose to be with friends and colleagues, socializing and working with people that understand and accept me as I am.

In my 30's, I started staying in one place longer and longer before finally settling in California. All of that relocating and not being settled served me well. Because of my vague beginnings, I thrive on connection now. I hunger for community, friendship, and the appreciation of one person for the other in a relationship. I've built long-term relationships personally and professionally that are mutually nourishing.

Now, whenever I do something, I go above and beyond. I have a deeper sense of being of service and I own that role proudly. Service is a feeling inside of me that's a soft excitement, like fireworks on the inside. It lights me up and radiates with an explosive force. I've started shining in new ways, exploring, being more adventurous because I've come into myself, allowing the growth I've experienced to shine even brighter. The burden of worrying about what others think has been lifted. My shoulders are light, my head is clear, and my heart is full.

My life has made me who I am today. Through the process of creation, I grew the roots I was seeking. I discovered that the way to fill the void of my early life was to go back inside myself, tie together the various tendrils, and nurture the once-tender shoots of my soul. This process built my strength upon a stable foundation. Now I share with others to help them build a solid base for what matters most to them.

The road I traveled was full of twists and turns. I learned that not living in a straight line from beginning to end is true for many others on their own path. Sharing our differences fills my heart with joy. **Now I know that I am not alone. We are each on a journey to find our own center.** Whatever roadblocks prevent us from finding our own homes, if we remember to go within, we'll never have to go without. Seek and you shall find your community.

Through my radio show, I help others find their center and balance in the journey of life. In my private financial practice, End The Red, I use my gifts of life's wisdom to guide my clients towards living debt-free and having their money support them and the life they are called to live.

Accepting the invitation to be part of this book gave me a chance to realize that despite a successful life, I have been hiding. As I've written this story, more pieces of my life have come together so I can move forward. Pieces of me that made me feel like I didn't belong have been healed because I now know that I belong in a different way. **I belong because in my heart, I'm whole. Now I belong to myself!**

When all is said and done, we're always working on something. As we continue to grow, obstacles will arise. When we clear away old challenges, we have space to work through new ones. Just like the military child of my youth, I've unpacked my old house, had my yard sale, and found my lighter home inside of me so I can keep moving on.

My life has taught me to carry my home with me wherever I go, because it lives in my heart. That kind of belonging is where we can all truly shine. We belong to our inner strength. We belong to our independence and our inter-dependence.

Now when people ask me, "Where you from?", I tell them I am from wherever I am in that moment. I have created roots where I feel comfortable and supported, where I am accepted, where I can feel whole and complete.

Ask yourself, "Where are you from?" When you can answer that question, you'll be where your home is...

Biography

Brandy Jones has always been an entrepreneur and educator. At the age of seven she started her first business, which planted the seeds of her first savings account and thus began a legacy of financial empowerment. Growing up in a military family, she relocated often and became adept at building new relationships with ease. It is this instant rapport that her diverse clientele shares with her today.

Ms. Jones accepts where her clients are without judgment. Having faced her own struggles with debt head-on, Ms. Jones learned to negotiate with creditors, manage a budget, and rebuild her savings. She has walked in the shoes of being heavily in debt and for her, filing bankruptcy was not an option. She wanted more than a quick fix.

Brandy Jones, CEO of End the Red, has a mission to empower others to live a financially sound life, and her vision is to educate the youth of today to be fiscally strong adults of tomorrow. Ms. Jones will assist those who are having difficulty with their credit and give them new choices through training and education. She has a unique way to get people to talk about finances, how they feel, and look at the big picture, and from there she can help them make sound decisions.

End the Red is a business where the client will feel empowered to continue to handle their finances in a more responsible matter. End the Red's purpose is to provide clients with a very personal and educational path on how to budget, how to maintain control with credit, and how to develop a savings plan.

Learn More...

brandy@endthered.com

www.EndtheRed.com

www.facebook.com/5DollarsBecauseUmatter

The Talk That Changed My Life
Karl Bobo

It was 1996 when I took a look in the mirror and did not like what I saw. I was in a job where I was supposed to be the "expert" in teaching others how to get the most out of life, however, what I saw in the mirror was a broken man in need of fixing himself. My job was unfulfilling, my personal life was unsatisfying, and my children needed me more than ever. When others I encountered found themselves in similar circumstances, they would oftentimes come to me for guidance, but who could I go to for help? I read just about every self-help book on the market, including the Bible, yet I still felt alone, empty, and badly in need of an attitude adjustment. I just didn't know exactly where to go for that adjustment.

I decided to get away from everything and everyone and go fishing. I am not saying that fishing is the solution, but it was the only thing I could think of at that moment and it turned out to be one of the best decisions of my life, preceded only by my decision to make Christ my Lord and Savior, my decision to marry my wife, and my decision to have and raise children. It was on that fishing trip that I had a talk that changed my life, and this same talk will change your life as well.

Over the remaining paragraphs, I will share with you what I learned from what I now call "The Talk."

There I was on a nice spring day in Mooresville, North Carolina, gliding along the glassy waters of Lake Norman in my boat, trying to find the perfect cove where I could stop and fish for the day. It was a Monday, and the lake was very still and quiet. I always like to fish this lake during the week because you don't have the amount of boat traffic, jet skiers, and water skiers that you do on the weekends, which makes for better fishing. As I travelled a few miles from the dock, I passed one boat early on, but I didn't see another boat over the next twenty minutes of riding. I came upon a beautiful cove that looked like no one had ever been there before. The water was clear and you could actually see fish jumping out of the water right by the boat. I decided that this would be a perfect place to fish, peaceful and quiet. As I dropped the anchor and turned off the engine to the boat, the only thing you could hear was the sound of bass playing in the water. It was so serene.

The Talk

After about four hours of fishing, and having caught zero fish, I decided to take a break for lunch. I still kept a few lines in the water just in case a fish was dumb enough to accidently run into my line and hook himself. The way things were going, I felt that was probably the only way I was going to catch a fish that day. As you can see, I really had a positive attitude. So I sat down, took out my sandwich, and took in the view. While taking in the view, I was reminded of a quote from Solomon that we had talked about at church the previous day. Proverbs 23:7 said something like, "As a person thinks of themselves, so are they." Those words just kept ringing in my mind while I sat in solitude. After an hour of just quiet (no fish), those words kept pounding on my mind. Then another quote came to my mind from an unknown author. "If it is to be, it is up to me."

These two statements led me to the talk that changed my life. You may have already guessed that The Talk was actually with myself. Talking to ourselves is not something that most of us want to be caught doing. As we get older, it can be misunderstood and some people will even think you are crazy. However, it may actually be one of the most helpful things that you can do to change your life. Studies have shown that people who grow up in positive environments where it is emphasized that the sky is the limit on what they can accomplish actually do better in most cases than people who grow up in negative environments where roadblocks and obstacles are the focus instead of opportunities. If you believe it, you can achieve it.

As I sat on the boat, I came to the conclusion that I had already read enough books, attended enough seminars, and heard enough motivational speakers to last me a lifetime.

The one thing that I was missing was taking personal responsibility to change the direction of my life. It was there on that boat that I said out loud, "Enough is enough."

The relationship between what we think, what we say, what we do, and what we become has been studied extensively. Dr. Doug Spenser stated, "When thoughts and words come from our own mind and mouth, they have just as much impact as they do when spoken by a significant other." I would take his statement one step farther and say that they actually have the potential to have more of an impact.

Mahatma Gandhi, the great philosopher, said, "Keep your thoughts positive because your thoughts become your words. Keep your words positive because your words become your behaviors. Keep your behaviors positive because your behaviors become your habits. Keep your habits positive because your habits become your values. Keep your values positive because your values become your identity." Gandhi paints for us a beautiful description of how our thoughts and words literally create who we are, and it is a strong endorsement for the value of constructive conversations you have with yourself.

Now let me be clear. It is extremely important that you actually talk out loud to yourself. The mind has a tendency to do what we actually say out loud. It is a similar methodology as writing things down. People who actually write things down (goals, to-do lists, etc.) have a higher percentage of accomplishments than those who don't write things down. It's that old adage that when we write things down or say them verbally, they become more real to us and we are more apt to act upon them.

Secondly, you have to be honest with yourself. I came to the conclusion on that boat that the real problem lay with me, and that is a tough pill to swallow. You have to ask yourself questions as if you were talking to someone else. You then have to follow up these tough questions with tough, transparent answers. If you are having weight problems, the conversation may go something like this: "I am obese. Why? I eat too much of the wrong food and don't exercise." What are you going to do about it? "I am going to eat only lean meats, fruits, and vegetables for one month. I am going to walk three miles a day for six days a week for the same one month. I am responsible for me.

I was one who struggled with my weight for years. Then I saw a picture of myself at my son's graduation and said, it is time for "The Talk." I must admit this was a tough conversation. For years, I would go to the doctor and the first thing he would say was, "Get on the scale."

I always said, "These weight charts are not designed for real people. I played football and lifted weights growing up. I surpassed the adult male ideal weight chart in high school." My favorite statement was, "I am not fat. I just have big bones." That was just an excuse.

After I had the talk with myself, I went online and looked at how much a person my age and height should weigh. After laughing myself to tears, I verbally announced to myself, "You are obese." I repeated the same words for a week. I then put into play an action plan that consisted of eating right and exercising to correct the problem. I am proud to say that I have been able to control my weight now for over five years.

It has been now over twenty years since I first had "The Talk" at the lake in 1996. Since that day, I have had too many blessings to describe. If you remember, I said that "The Talk" was the fourth best decision I had made in my life. It followed my decision to follow God, my decision to marry my wife, and my decision to have and raise children. Do you see the connection? They were all decisions. There comes a time in life that we have to all stop wandering through life and make a decision.

Choose to come out of hiding and shine. Choose to embrace life. Choose to have "The Talk."

Biography

Karl Bobo is a bestselling author, entrepreneur, life/ business coach and a dynamic speaker. He is the CEO and founder of Choose 2 Embrace Life, an organization designed to help people see the positives in life, recognize its splendor and get the maximum benefit from it. Karl is a dynamic motivational speaker and financial business executive in Northern California. He has over twenty years of experience in working with business professionals, business owners, individuals, groups, and organizations in the development of skills and the mindset needed to maximize one's efforts in life. Karl is extremely passionate about helping to guide people into experiencing life differently. It is necessary to embrace the one chance we get at life.

E-xperience (the best of life)

M-eaning (a life with value)

B-righten (positive outlook)

R-omance (find the happiness)

A-ttitude (determines success)

C-elebrate (why not?)

E-njoy (all life brings)

Karl has reached out to corporate America and pulled out some of the best coaches and trainers available, and they have over 100 years of combined experience. Specifically, he has drawn from a pool of individuals with unique skillsets in the area of "execution." Karl has identified a major drawback in the training and development of most individuals. Most organizations do a good job at telling people "what" to do, but they fall short of helping people develop the necessary skills of "how" to execute. This is one area that the Choose 2 Embrace Life team places great emphasis on.

Mr. Bobo is a dynamic motivational speaker who draws on his vast experience in corporate leadership, entrepreneurship, one-on-one coaching, sports, parenting, and marriage to truly connect with his clients. Karl and his team provide workshops and follow up coaching to ensure the implementation of the valuable information and principles learned. Karl has a passion for life like no other. When talking with him, you get the feeling that the "glass is always half full." This is not to say that he has not faced obstacles like most people face, but that he has developed a different way of turning what others believe are challenges and setbacks into the very thing that launches people to greatness.

Karl is a strong believer in the control of the mind. Our attitude plays a larger role than what people actually believe in our overall success in life. He has often said, "Before you can get people to act right, you have to first get them to think right." He also chose the numeral 2 in his business name as opposed to the more grammatically correct "to" because he wanted everyone to understand that life is not simply about your individual development and success. We all have a responsibility to bring someone else along with us. CEO of Choose 2 Embrace Life!

Learn More...

Choose2embracelife.com

Email: karl@choose2embracelife.com

Phone: 510-292-5282

Surrender to the Light
Carla Puentes

Just as a mountain hides the warmth of the rising sun, we, too, can hide the gifts bestowed within us from the world. We are all born with a purpose. I believe it is our responsibility to discover it, embrace it, and fulfill it.

Living our purpose provides freedom, success, and joy. So why are there so few people doing it? What is your opinion? Are you living your purpose? I have spent the majority of my adult life either being frustrated at not knowing what mine was or thinking that what I discovered was too insignificant to actually believe it was the one God had picked for me. I mean, seriously? Touching peoples' hearts through business? It felt as corny as it sounds. It took years of confirmation for me to decide to embrace it. Now I can confidently and joyfully say that I see, hear, know, and feel that the purpose of my life is to passionately love and live as I positively impact peoples' hearts and lives and fill them with hope. My purpose doesn't only apply to my business of helping people with their marriages and emotional and physical health, but also in my home, with my family, and with my friends.

I can now acknowledge that I have a gift that can change peoples' lives, and I can feel the freedom and joy that comes from that acknowledgment. You may be wondering what shifted for me. I'll tell you with the hope that you will embrace and surrender to the light being called forth within you.

My favorite quote is one from a famous teaching given by Marianne Williamson. She said, "We ask ourselves, who am I to be brilliant, gorgeous, talented, and fabulous? Actually, who are you not to be? You are a child of God. Your playing small does not serve the world. There is nothing enlightened about shrinking so that other people won't feel insecure around you. We were born to make manifest the glory of God that is within us, and as we let our own light shine, we unconsciously give other people permission to do the same."

I understood the message well...pertaining to you. But it took me years to get out of God's way to use me in the way I believe He had in mind.

For years, I have stifled my greatness. You see, instead of understanding and truly grasping that I was born with amazing talents and gifts and greatness and that I was gifted these to use for the benefit of others, as well as my own, I was focused on being humble. I would like to look at this word: humble. I always believed that being humble meant not being conceited or thinking too highly of oneself. However, I had a conflict in my mind because I knew I was talented and I had a desire for a successful business.

I had an even deeper conflict about people not approving of me if I truly showed up and shined. What if I give it all I have and no one likes my service or me? But things started to change the older I became as I realized I couldn't stand the mediocre me who was playing small. I couldn't stand not living "my" life. I couldn't take not loving myself anymore.

Now, as I decided to try out my wings, I ran into my second obstacle: fear of not being enough. Even though I had been learning, studying, and apprenticing in my field for fifteen years, along with the PhD of real life I'd earned, I didn't think I knew enough to have a business and actually get paid real money for it. I believe in expertise and excellence, but I took it too far and expected perfection within myself. So as crazy as it sounds, I went from recognizing my amazing talents but being afraid to really shine to being scared to death that I wasn't really as gifted as I had thought. So I was in the same place: stuck.

Perspective is based on past experience, not on reality. Sometimes you need to change your perspective. It was time for me to change the lens I was viewing my life through. I also needed to change my perspective of how others see me. We all try to project the best version of ourselves. There's more pressure on us than ever before, especially with social media, to present a polished image. We all want to be accepted.

As my perspective changed, my life started to shift. I started listening for God to speak to me and I started hearing more positive messages than I had been telling myself, things like, "You are enough." I started to focus on how I could serve others and started to recognize that although I had been sharpening my skills for years, the gifts I have were given to me at birth. I have had access to these gifts my entire life, whether I chose to use them consistently or not.

Slowly the true meaning of being humble or having humility was revealed to me. Humility is not only thinking too much of oneself, but it is also not thinking too little of oneself. It is simply not thinking of oneself. It is about stepping into a true place of service for others and realizing that I am simply a vessel that light can shine through, if I allow it.

In the Holy Bible, in Matthew 5:14-16, the verses read, "You are the light of the world. A city set on a hill cannot be hidden. Nor do men light a lamp and put it under a barrel but instead on a lampstand. Let your light so shine before men that they may see your praiseworthy, noble, and good deeds and recognize and honor and praise and glorify God."

I am able to see so clearly with hindsight how I decided to light my lamp and then was so afraid to put it on a lampstand that I just blew it out.

I didn't gain anything by being afraid. Being scared only incapacitates us. It hinders our ability to step into greatness. When a good man or woman lines up his purpose with action and overcomes fear, the world is the one who benefits. All the negative thoughts in my head or the hindrances keeping me from sharing my light come from a selfish place because the focus is on me. John Wayne once said that courage is being scared to death and saddling up anyway. It's okay to be afraid, but to shine, we must remember to have courage and do what it takes to not let fear cripple us.

Do you have any excuses or belief systems holding you back from greatness? Do you think you don't know enough or aren't smart enough? Maybe you think you need to lose a few pounds first, need to accumulate some more money, need to be married, need to get unmarried, need to learn more, need another course... Maybe you just need to surrender to the light living within you and step onto the path before you with confidence, knowing you were born with a purpose and the core gifts needed to fulfill that purpose.

The awesome thing about light is that you can have a room full of it and have a huge black spot in the room and it doesn't affect the light, but if you have a pitch black room and only have one small candle light, it takes over the darkness. It doesn't matter if I am only a small vessel of light. What matters is that I keep glowing and affecting the world around me.

How can you or I justify not impacting as many lives as we are able to? You are capable of so much more than you can think or imagine if you will only allow yourself to be used by God and be a vessel of light and love.

Watch for signs of resistance. There are sneaky patterns that you cannot always see yourself. Look for these patterns of hiding. They may even appear as things that need to be done. For me, that usually looks like dishes in the sink, laundry that could be done, or really any household chore, because of a deeply-rooted belief taught to me as a child that my most important job is taking care of my home. The problem with that is that I am not only a wife and mom, but I am also a businesswoman. Deciding that I must deep clean my house is definitely a sneaky self-sabotaging behavior when I have a business deal I should be making. This doesn't mean that I should not ever do domestic duties. However, I need to be aware of when and why I do them. I have realized that it makes much more sense for me to hire someone to clean my house and make the money in my business to pay for it.

What are ways you may be resisting or sabotaging your greatness? Too much time on Facebook? Do you avoid making or accepting phone calls? Do you prefer hiding behind a computer to avoid face to face interactions with people you need to be interacting with? You have to really step back and stop and observe automated reactions.

It is also imperative to have at least one person who completely supports you in following and living your purpose. It is best when this is someone you are in an intimate relationship with, someone who supports you in all areas of your life. My hope for you is that if you don't have this kind of relationship that you do the work necessary to develop one.

However, you can find someone who supports you outside of friends and family. Just make sure this person can and will be there to believe in you when you have lost the belief in yourself or even your faith in God. Please remember, it is your responsibility to find this person, even paying them if necessary. It is not okay to decide to be a victim of walking your path alone. God designed us to need others. If you feel alone, do whatever it takes to get support, even if it means hiring a coach or joining a mastermind. The more support you create for yourself, the better!

I challenge you to surrender to your purpose and be a vessel of light. Share the gifts you were given at birth that are yours alone to give, because no one can do it for you. Quit making excuses, don't live in fear, watch for sneaky self-sabotaging behaviors, create a support system for yourself, and make the difference you were called to make!

Biography

Carla Puentes grew up on a cattle ranch in Texas as the youngest of five siblings. Now as a mother of five and with a strongly-rooted passion for family, she works with people around the world to heal their broken relationships and she has a gift for finding the corrections needed to help people heal their intimate relationships. She has a B.A. in Education and is a certified Life Language Communication Coach, Certified Couples Coach, and Health Coach. She has worked doing transformational and team building work for over fifteen years.

Carla is a national speaker and experiential leadership facilitator. She has not only done this work with individuals and couples, but also for network marketing teams and hospitals.

Carla's greatest joy is helping people learn how to have amazing relationships with the people around them. She is passionate about her work because after having a failed relationship herself, she understands the pain and cost involved. She has spent years growing from that experience - or opportunity, as she calls it - so she can now help others thrive in their relationships.

She primarily works with Christian couples who are struggling in their first or second marriages and still have children living in their home. These couples usually do not want to end their marriage, but do not know how to make it work. They sometimes feel trapped and believe they are destined to live in an unfulfilled relationship. Typically they have a push/pull relationship where one of the partners feels they can never do or be enough and the other partner actually agrees with them. Carla feels so much joy when these couples discover how to live in harmony with their mates and children and/or stepchildren and extended families.

She would be honored to have a conversation with you. Feel free to contact her:

Learn More...

Carla@carlapuentes.com

www.carlapuentes.com

www.facebook.com/carlapuentes

Entrepreneur by Nature
Sarah Calhoun

At first I was a stealth entrepreneur. I did the usual kid things: Girl Scout cookies door-to-door (back when people thought nothing of little girls going around ringing doorbells of strangers), and then I sent away for greeting cards to also sell door-to-door, although I hated doing it. My mom ended up buying most of those and used them up over the next decade. When my neighbor and I wanted to learn to knit, off we went to the doorbells, looking for a lady who could teach us. In college I did election canvassing, once again knocking on strangers' doors, and then getting into heated political debates with them on their doorsteps or in their living rooms. After college, I hitchhiked around the western U.S. and then around Western Europe, and I always found hospitality and welcome. During a summer spent on a bike trip through England and France, there was yet more ringing of doorbells - this time to ask people if they would "put the kettle on for tea" for us. This request and routine were so instantly familiar to nearly everyone we met that once again we got offered places to stay, meals, rides, clothing, jobs.... At one point I remember thinking this could be a reasonable way to spend your life, just knocking on people's doors and letting them give you things.

In retrospect, I identified this as the first stage of being, or becoming, an entrepreneur: getting comfortable with it, feeling natural about it. All those years of doorbell-ringing, these days supplanted and enhanced by social media and other electronic methods, reaching the point of "why not?" In subsequent years there was more political canvassing, both door-to-door and by phone, and other forms of cold-calling. I have never gotten comfortable with the term "cold-calling" - it is so off-putting. But looking back I realized that I've done plenty of it.

In my working life, I also discovered plenty of entrepreneurship. You know how they say, the best job is the one you create for yourself? That has certainly been true for me, although at first I didn't realize I was doing it. I was so far in hiding in my entrepreneurial nature, I was hidden even from myself! But I began to notice that I always did best in work situations that I had somehow fallen into, rather than ones that involved résumés and interviews and job descriptions. My favorite form of entrepreneurship in those days was working freelance: for painting and handyman work, for reviewing legal and academic documents, for writing and photography and leading hikes. How I fell into all those situations and a few more besides is probably a novel in itself, but they all did present themselves, and all I had to do was say, "Yes! I can do that!" - and of course, for it actually to be true. These days, with Craigslist and TaskRabbit and so on, many people are getting good at the "yes" part.

Eventually in every entrepreneur's life there is the recognition moment, the "Oh, so that's what I've been doing" time. Despite taking courses in enterprise development and community building in college, that was not my recognition time. And all my years of freelance work were also still not enough of a clue to me. What finally helped me recognize my entrepreneurial nature was being tasked not only with creating my own job, but with creating and funding my whole department. Essentially, the challenge was, "Bring in the money for it and you can have a job." These kinds of opportunities can be created, but in my case, it was another right-place, right-time scenario. Having done that once for a research department, I realized I liked it and I did it again for a service organization, and again for a team of consultants. Then I kept on doing it, for my own consulting and for my current enterprises.

But by far my biggest entrepreneurial challenge was taking care of my father in his final years. Caregiving as entrepreneurship is kind of a surprise equation, but if you think about it, caregiving uses all the entrepreneurial muscles you have built up - and then some. You have to take initiative, you have to get out in front of your market, you have to keep on top of new developments in your field. There is paperwork and repetition and relationship-building with complementary entities like doctors and insurance programs and care facilities. You have to hire and fire people, you have to manage many kinds of processes. And the buck stops right there, in front of your face. You do what's necessary, when it needs to be done, and you keep going. If you have not come out of hiding as an entrepreneur when you take on the first task of what will eventually become caregiving, you cannot help but recognize your inner entrepreneur by the time it is over.

And that's really a great thing, because **entrepreneurship is fundamentally an affirming process: it's how you learn what you are made of.** Sure, plenty of jobs are challenging too, and you learn a lot about yourself in the course of fulfilling any responsibility. But when it's your livelihood also on the line, and especially when it's the livelihoods of other people as well, whether employees or care recipients, there is nothing either more satisfying or, at times, more terrifying. Sometimes you find yourself thinking, "Why me? Why am I in this position?" and then you remember, "Oh yeah. Because I can. Because I'm good at it. Because, who else?" And that's when all your lessons and talents as an entrepreneur, even when they were hidden from you, come into focus. You're comfortable with it, you say yes, and you recognize your skills.

Once this all happens, it's time to put those entrepreneurial skills into the service of something very fundamental: your dreams. Falling into entrepreneurship is great, being thrown in at the deep end is even better, but when you have the opportunity to be deliberate about what you will use your skills for, it's magical. When you know that you will be able to support yourself wherever you go, you can start looking for the doors that are opening to you, rather than trying to knock down doors or make doors out of walls. I've tried all those access methods, and believe me, open doors are the best. **Being entrepreneurial means being open to possibilities rather than feeling locked in or tied down**. Being entrepreneurial means you can always use the best of yourself, for yourself, rather than giving it away or letting someone else get the benefit of your talents. **Being entrepreneurial, you get to determine the terms of your own life.** Sure, sometimes those terms are twelve-hour days and no vacations. But that is where the shine part comes in. **You get to shine by developing entrepreneurship so that it serves you rather than you being its servant.**

The most important part of the entrepreneurial manifesto, after all, is dreams. What is your dream, and what will you do to put it into effect? And, in the service of coming out of hiding, what have you already done to develop your ability to make your dreams happen? Remember, our dreams are not just random thoughts. We have them for a reason. Your dreams are a combination of your own skills, interests, and history. In some traditions they are called "what you were put on earth to do." Even if you don't have a belief system that includes that sense of destiny, you may still have a feeling of being compelled or drawn to a particular kind of activity or project. I found it interesting to learn, not so long ago, that the role of the Three Fates, in both Greek and Roman mythology, was to determine the *consequences* of our actions, not the actions themselves. If you look at destiny or fate in that way, entrepreneurialism becomes almost mandatory. What do you think the consequences would be of doing what you are drawn to do, versus not doing that thing or making that choice?

Since graduating from caregiving, I have had an opportunity to reflect on my own dreams as well as to recognize my journey and my talents. It has become my mission to help people realize their dreams, and do it in a way that nurtures and supports their health and happiness rather than becoming a drain on their life. I support caregivers in taking care of themselves while they take care of others, and I support entrepreneurs who are fulfilling their dreams and wanting to remain sane in the process. I think everyone has an important dream, and everyone also is an entrepreneur by nature. Sometimes it takes a while in our lives to recognize it, but once you do, looking back over your life as I did over mine, you can identify the various milestones in your entrepreneurial journey and know where you are in it and what support you need at that point in time. The bottom line, which entrepreneurs are very fond of, is that you can get to shine as an entrepreneur in service of your dream, and by doing so you can serve yourself and others powerfully. Here are my top five tips for tapping into your entrepreneurial spirit and shining:

1. **Take stock of your life**. Have you had some of the same kinds of experiences I had, that I didn't recognize as entrepreneurial until much later? Think about your life as if you were writing a biography. What would you recognize about yourself if you were someone else looking in? Ask other people what they think your greatest talents and gifts are. Many times we don't recognize the value of something we have lived with all our lives - namely, ourselves!

2. **Focus on your dream.** What do you feel called to do, what would be your purpose in life if you weren't so busy doing all your daily maintenance activities? Those aren't going to go away, but there are ways to configure your time to make room for pursuing your dreams even in the midst of your current reality.

3. **Prioritize your self-care.** If you do not serve yourself, you will not be able to serve others. It's that simple. It doesn't have to take a lot of time during the day, but spend some time figuring out the essentials for you and set up routines that will let you meet those basic needs. No matter what else you are doing, this one effort will pay off in major ways in your life.

4. **Get real.** Get real with yourself, with your money and time, with your family, and with your past and future. Start talking about your dreams, telling people what you want to be about. This will not in itself create that reality, but it is a step in the direction of coming out of hiding. You never know what will come your way as a result of this process!

5. **Get good help.** For every stage of the entrepreneurial journey, there are coaching programs, people, courses. Sometimes cities or counties have departments or programs that help people start or expand businesses. Sometimes our dreams are not about a business, but some other kind of project. Whatever your dream is, start exploring what support is out there, what kinds of assistance already exist, and what you could both make use of as well as provide in that arena.

It is my honor to help people identify, focus and follow their dreams, and if you are on that path, I would be very happy to hear from you.

Biography

I have supported myself for over thirty-five years on self-generated income, starting businesses involving service, sales, consulting, research, and labor management. With Masters' degrees in public health and in city and regional planning, I have led research teams, set up service organizations, organized consultants, and done individual consulting. All of my professional work, in both large and small organizations, has been on an entrepreneurial basis. I have been bringing in the money to fund my team along with doing and leading the work itself. I have received grant-based funding and start-up capital and I have also had nothing at all to begin with. Most recently, I have been a family caregiver and became involved in supporting other caregivers with information, encouragement, and training. All of these efforts have taught me about enterprise development as well as the care and feeding of entrepreneurs, what we need to stay the course and make the dream succeed.

Learn More...

www.busywomendream.com

Bringing Your 'A' Game™:
Nine Steps to Live and Work on Purpose
Toti Cadavid

Have you ever found yourself asking, "Why am I living this way?" What moves you to do the things you do or be with the people you have chosen to be with? Why are you in your chosen field, job, or overall position? These are all excellent questions to ponder. I believe that most of us waste our lives in a rush, living it on autopilot and we seldom stop to question why we do what we do. I'd like to share a bit of my story with the intention that if your life resembles how I once lived, then do know that life could be truly fulfilled by implementing just a few changes.

It wasn't until after my husband and I miraculously survived a car accident that I started to ask myself the key fundamental questions about how I was living my life and what types of relationships I was having with the people I loved and cared about the most. Facing death forced me to look at the type of legacy I would have left behind had I died. The answers to those questions were devastatingly sad. I understood that I was letting everyone I loved down because I allowed my business and my career to come before everything and everyone else. I was a workaholic for whom even those I loved the most - my kids and husband - came after my professional responsibilities. I was too busy for my friends and for my extended family, and definitely too busy to even get sick or take care of myself.

After much reflection and many coaching sessions, I also realized that, just like an addict, I was living my life in search of the next "fix". I would work so hard to achieve the next goal, thinking that it would finally bring that stage of happiness I was searching for, but when I got there, the satisfaction never lasted. I mistakenly assumed that this feeling was due to the fact that I had not reached a big enough goal that would provide me with long-lasting happiness. I would then set an even bigger goal for myself and immediately start striving towards it. This went on and on, and all the while I was telling myself that I would be able to devote myself to all the things and people that were also important to me, as soon as I found that stage of great success and happiness. Just like that, I had fallen into a never-ending spiral, searching for what I now refer to as "empty success", the type of success that could never bring true and lasting happiness because it is all about reaching goals that originated from one's head instead of our heart.

In the midst of all that guilt I felt about the mess I created out of my life, the most critical "why" question bubbled to the surface: *"Why did I allow the importance of my work to take over my life?"* The very painful answer was that I went after success because it was the only way I could connect with my mother, all in the name of earning her love and respect. My mother has always been a very admired and esteemed businesswoman, but work was always her first priority. She worked tirelessly, day in and day out. Growing up, I resented and criticized her for never taking time for herself, for failing to nurture relationships with her children or friends, and for not being truly present, loving, or available. Nonetheless, I wanted her love and respect and had found a way to earn it...or so I thought.

Unfortunately, I was repeating my mother's pattern and doing exactly the same she did with my life and to those I cared about. I worked intensely during most of my waking hours, leaving very little time for anything or anyone else. Becoming aware of what was driving my actions was very difficult. I was filled with guilt and at the same time I was able to recognize all that I had missed and wanted to have in my life. It was as if my whole life flashed before my eyes, giving me the clarity to recognize what and who was important to me. That was the moment when a very powerful inner desire to live life to the fullest was born. I could not wait to truly love and feel loved, to have joy in my life, to find a new career direction, to work differently, to get balanced...to feel alive. I was awakened and absolutely ready to see the habits I needed to change, the wrongs I needed to right, and the relationships I needed to repair.

"Happiness is not a state to arrive at, but a manner of traveling."

~ Margaret Lee Runbeck

I therefore set another lofty goal, and this one would be the biggest, most difficult, and most important of my life: **to finally live and experience a meaningful and fulfilling life.** Immediately, several obstacles jumped out at me. First, I didn't even know what it *meant* to live a meaningful life, and then the all-too-common fears of change and failure showed up. I didn't know where to start or how to overcome all of those challenges, but the one thing I had was sheer determination along with a robust inner desire to get more out of life. So, after a lengthy inner-exploration phase with the help of several programs, coaching sessions, and any book on the subject I could get my hands on, I was able to understand what I needed to do. Learning by trial and error became part of my daily routine as I implemented the new concepts I was gaining.

When you start changing, everything around you changes...

It is extremely rewarding to see that when you change, everything and everyone around you changes. When you enter into a place of inner alignment, you are able to clarify your values, understand the source of your misalignments, re-discover your fortes and passions, and find out how you can create a life that reflects your innermost desires. You are also able to organize your life around your priorities, build strong and healthy relationships with your loved ones, and find your true north. Even the important relationships in your professional life change and you also become a stronger, more effective leader at work.

The miracles that happen when one lives a life of meaning and with a new level of awareness one can stop passing those mistakes down through generations. Living fully and fulfilled and helping others do the same became my inspiration; I began to dedicate my life to help others go from chaos and confusion to clarity and happiness. I developed a nine-step process for gaining clarity and inner alignment that continues to help me and others create the types of lives we want to live. This process even allowed me to understand that I had become disconnected from the marketing and branding career I had dedicated so much for twenty years because just as it happens for product brands, the disconnection in individuals also happens when we (the "product") can't deliver on our brand promise. To live life fully, we must truly know who we are, what impact we want to have on others, and then build systems that allow that brand promise to be delivered in every area of our life.

Even though so many people have an inner desire to change some aspect of their lives, most won't even try because they have no idea how to make real change happen or they are afraid of the path ahead. Do know, however, that the possibility of feeling and living fulfilled is your birthright. We just allow many layers of outdated beliefs, guilt, and sorrow to steal that joy from us. If there is any part of you feeling unease and your inner voice is whispering that there must be something more to life than what you are experiencing, I invite you to join me in the nine-step process I discovered through my own transformation. This is the same transformative process I successfully use with my clients to help them develop their "A-Game Self", or the best version of themselves. To ease the journey, we use a series of questionnaires and exercises for each step during my program, but you can still gain clarity and alignment if you answer the following questions in a profound way:

Bringing Your "A" Game™

STEP 1: ASSESS: WHAT'S THE REALITY OF MY SITUATION?

STEP 2: AUTHENTICIZE: WHO AM I?

STEP 3: ALIGN: HOW DO I WANT TO BE EXPERIENCED BY OTHERS IN MY VARIOUS ROLES?

STEP 4: ANCHOR: WHO & WHAT AM I BEING CALLED TO BE?

STEP 5: AIM: WHAT DO I WANT FOR MY LIFE?

STEP 6: AWARE: WHAT DO I NEED TO CHANGE, EMBRACE, AND/OR DEVELOP TO BECOME WHO I WANT TO BE?

STEP 7: AVERT: WHAT IS KEEPING ME FROM BEING AND CREATING WHAT I WANT?

STEP 8: ACHIEVE: HOW DO I BECOME AND ACCOMPLISH WHO I'M BEING CALLED TO BE AND DO?

STEP 9: ACTIVATE: HOW CAN I CONSISTENTLY EXPRESS WHO I TRULY AM AS I BUILD AN EMPOWERING BRAND?

Activating alignment and clarity in my own life ignited a passion to help others create lives they could only dream about before. Now it's time for you to reflect on your own life. If you are not feeling fulfilled, it is time to discover and remove what has been holding you back and share with the world the highest expression of who you are. We are here to make a difference in the lives of others by being who we truly are and finding joy in every situation. The way you live your life is what matters. The question is, are you willing to shine your light brightly and live fully?

I hope that you can also reap the rewards of intentionally living a life of ease and fulfillment, of knowing what's important to you and then designing a life around it. I promise it will be worth your investment of time and effort to make the critical self-discoveries that allow you to become empowered to create a truly harmonious and meaningful life experience. Join my blog, get my free gift, and find more information on this subject at www.essencialize.com.

Biography

Toti Cadavid is a seasoned multicultural marketing and communications strategist with expertise in both domestic and international markets who, after a near-death experience, was moved to reconsider her career in terms of the impact she was having on the world. She became a bestselling author, speaker, trainer, and certified coach. She launched Essencialize, a conscious branding and leadership development company that focuses on helping top performers lead better teams and companies by working on their self-awareness, emotional intelligence, and true inner brand, and ensuring that everyone in the organization is aligned and connected to their and the organization's values. Toti empowers her clients to discover their "why", their internal motivation, so that as aligned individuals, they can reach higher levels of success, balance, meaning, and purpose in their lives and careers. Toti is a co-author of *Pebbles in the Pond: Wave Four* which reached bestseller status in several countries.

Toti spent the first half of her nineteen-year marketing career in corporate America designing and implementing fully integrated local and global marketing and communications efforts for companies such as AT&T's Media One and The Hallmark Channel. Then, from 2002-2012, Toti was president and CEO of Xcelente, a cross-cultural marketing, branding, and communications agency that launched or re-built over 52 brands in the Hispanic marketplace. Under her leadership, she provided the agency's clients with communication solutions that incorporated social, ethnic, and cultural nuances into all *marketing, branding, public relations, community outreach, public information, and advertising* initiatives.

Toti has always been deeply committed to giving back to the community and she has held leadership positions in a number of local and national business and civic organizations. Toti currently sits on the boards of the Denver Metro Chamber of Commerce, the Colorado Health Foundation, Denver International Airport's Management Advisory Council, Junior Achievement, and El Pomar Foundation's Denver Council. Toti was recognized in 2005 as one of the nation's Top

Latina Business Entrepreneurs by *Hispanic* magazine, as a finalist by the Colorado Rockies for the Hispanic Heritage Leadership Award, and by *The Denver Business Journal* as one of the "Top Forty Under 40" business leaders in Colorado. In 2006, Toti received the Businesswoman of the Year award by the Denver Hispanic Chamber of Commerce, the Minority Small Business Champion Award by the SBA, and she was named a "Woman of Distinction" by the Girl Scouts in 2007.

Toti holds a Bachelor's degree in International Business, a Master's degree in Marketing, another Master's degree in Management & Organizational Development, and a Certificate in Entrepreneurship, all from the University of Colorado. Toti is also a graduate of Harvard's Kennedy School of Government Executive Management Program, the 2004 Leadership Program of the Rockies, the 2005 Leadership Denver program, the 2005 National Hispana Leadership Institute, and the 2005 Dartmouth University Tuck Minority Business Executive Program. She holds a QSCA coaching certification and is a licensed master-level graduate of the Avatar Self-Empowerment Training Program.

Toti, a native of Colombia, lives in Denver, Colorado with her husband Luis Colón and their three children.

Learn More...

tcadavid@essencialize.com

www.essencialize.com

https://www.facebook.com/toticadavidessencialize

https://www.linkedin.com/in/toti-cadavid-2a8248

Let's Make Selling (and Life) Easier!
Leslie Ellis

A while back, I discovered that I often make things harder than they need to be. Clearly this is not done consciously so when I realized it, I was quite surprised. I thought back to a number of times when I had done this and became angry at myself. I quickly realized this wouldn't accomplish anything and decided that from that point on, I would stop doing this. Of course, this is sometimes easier said than done! I'm happy to say that, although I occasionally have the inclination to make things hard, now I catch myself and ask myself how to make it easier. It is amazing what a difference it makes.

Funny enough, when I sat down to start writing this chapter, I worked myself into a tizzy. When I signed on, I didn't quite understand the premise. My journey from coming out of hiding to shining? I've never been one to hide so clearly I have nothing to write about, right? Oh no, this is going to be hard - really hard, because writing is not one of my strengths! Or maybe not. I am writing about something I love and have a grand passion for: sales. I can talk sales all day and all night with no effort whatsoever, so writing should be easy too. Once I changed my mindset, sure enough, the words started to flow.

My hope is to help YOU come out of hiding when it comes to sales so you can shine! Sales can be easy!

Guess what? By thinking about sales differently, writing became easy because I'm talking about something I'm at expert at and something I love. You love your business, you're an expert, and you are helping people, so doing your business is easy for you. If you think about sales differently, it will be easier. I promise!

You might be wondering what makes me qualified to teach sales. Well, I've been doing it for thirty-four years! I started working with large clients such as Sony, Oracle, and Charles Schwab. Then I moved to medium-sized companies, and nine years ago I started working with small companies and individuals. I've learned what works and what doesn't and tweaked it along the way as things change. Because I've worked with so many different companies in different industries and different people in different positions, I'm in a unique place to help others. I can't say I've seen it all, but I've definitely seen and experienced a lot!

I have a deep desire to help entrepreneurs become comfortable with selling. So many of them have a fear of sales, often almost a hatred. We all dislike those pushy, hard sell, "salesy" people, don't we? Many entrepreneurs go in the exact opposite direction and don't practice any (or few) sales skills because they are afraid of being perceived as one of those awful people. Keep in mind: It is very difficult to have a wildly successful business if you can't sell. My motto (if you will) is "You can't serve if you can't sell". It really is true.

I discovered the way to make sales easier! Being a good salesperson really takes only two actions:

1.   Connecting with people

2.   Having conversations

Have you ever met someone and they immediately start talking about their product or service before they know anything about you? I call it the barfing syndrome. They "barf" all over you with a non-stop monologue about their product or service. This does not make people want to buy from you. In fact, it usually sends people running away. You need to make a connection with a potential client by getting to know them. Ask questions and LISTEN to the answers. Don't just ask about business; find out about who they are. Do they have kids? Are they planning a vacation this summer? Have they been to the movies lately? Of course, you also want to know about their business and what they might need. Keep in mind, you don't want to grill them about their business, you just want to...

Simply have a conversation. Stop trying to find clients! Yes, you read that correctly. Just talk with people and show an interest in them. When you talk with a person you have just met like they are a friend, it relaxes them and they will most likely answer your questions. This enables you to get to know them a little bit to determine if there might be a fit for the two of you.

Why do you want to establish a connection? People buy from people they know, like, and trust. This can't happen until you've had some conversation. Take it one step at a time. Don't rush into trying to sign them as a client. Get to know them first so you can determine if you even want them as a client.

Yes, it really is that simple! However, I understand that simple is not necessarily easy. Have you heard the expression "He's a born salesman"? It is true that some people have a gift for sales AND sales is a learned skill. Everyone can learn to be good at sales. Everyone is not an exaggeration. The secret is wanting to be good at sales. Rather than fearing or dreading sales, embrace it. Make it easy so you can shine. I'm going to show you how.

The first step to make selling easier is to have a clearly defined target market. Who exactly is your ideal client? Many people don't want to do that because they feel it excludes people. In fact, it draws more people to you because they know you might be the right person to help them. It also makes it easier for people to refer you.

Once you get to know them a little bit and you have agreed to talk about your product or service, you need to present your product or service in a compelling way so it is desirable to the prospect. You want to talk about the benefits of your product or service. You need to find out what benefits they are looking for (again by having a conversation and asking questions) and present with those top-of-mind. This makes it easy for them to say yes to working with you.

I am continually surprised how often people don't ask me to do business with them after they have told me about their product or service - and I do mean directly ask, no pussy footing around! Some (many?) people believe that if what you are offering is right, the potential client will tell you they want to buy. Maybe...maybe not. If you want to have a wildly successful business, you need to ask people to do business with you. This might sound hard, but it isn't. It's actually quite easy if you have made that connection.

Now for the R word: Rejection. This is a place where I see people making sales really hard. They don't ask for business or sometimes even for the appointment because they don't want to hear "no". Of course, we don't want to be pushy and we certainly don't want to do anything resembling a hard sell. In thirty-four years, I have never, ever done a hard sell. It's not necessary if you have done your job correctly. Let's be clear: asking someone to do business with you is NOT being pushy if you ask nicely. "How does the work I do sound to you?" is not being pushy. "Would you like to get started next week?" is not being pushy. "Do you want the cream in the 5 oz. or 10 oz. jar?" is not being pushy. It's simply asking how they want to proceed. It's asking them to do business with you.

Of course, every person you talk with isn't going to say yes. People are going to say no for many different reasons. Although it's obvious, I'm going to say it anyway: you aren't the right person for everyone you meet and not everyone is the right client for you. You really only want to work with your ideal clients.

There are two ways to avoid rejection:

1. Hire someone to do the sales for you.

2. Close your business and go back to corporate.

Seriously, you are 100% guaranteed to hear no - over and over if you are in business for any length of time. You need to find a way to be okay with it. You can try the "Go for No" approach, knowing that each no gets you closer to a yes. The best suggestion I have heard is to keep a list or a journal of everything good that happens to you each day, business and/or personal. Then when you get that no, you can look at what you have written and be reminded that lots of good things have happened. It does soften the blow.

What it all comes down to is mindset. Selling is a lot like life. If you think it is hard, it will be hard. If you think it will be easy, it will be easy.

If sales is where you are hiding and/or if you would like to shine in your business, I would love to give you my free report, "The One Thing You Can Do Now to Immediately Make More Money", at http://www.savvysellingnow.com/the-one-thing-you-can-do-now-to-immediately-make-more-money/

Happy Selling!

Biography

Leslie Ellis successfully negotiated her first sales job at the tender age of ten when she convinced her neighbor that she could take care of their newborn baby. Not many youngsters would have that maturity, but she was - and still is - confident in her talents and abilities.

Leslie started her professional sales career selling to large organizations such as Oracle, Sony, and Charles Schwab, which she did for twenty years. This experience spanned every level of management and many sales processes. She was awarded multiple honors, including Gold Club three years in a row. Gold Club requires over $500K in sales per year. During this time, she also earned an MBA.

Having grown up in a household with teachers, Leslie had no formal sales training when she began her career. She built all of her businesses from the ground up, learning all phases of selling by trial and error. From knocking on doors and cold calling to many of the most popular approaches to selling, she learned and practiced all of them.

Leslie found her next adventure working with small-to-medium-sized companies, where she learned new approaches to selling. In the end, she found that building relationships was the most compelling and exciting aspect of selling.

In 2014 she launched Savvy Selling NOW! She combined more than thirty years of sales experience, her passions for sales, people, and fun into a coaching and training business for entrepreneurs.

Learn More...

leslie@savvysellingnow.com

www.linkedin.com/in/leslieellis

www.facebook.com/leslieinsuranceguru

www.twitter.com/leslieellis

Wandering Girl, Abundant Woman
Carmell Pelly

I felt different as a young girl. My family never treated me any differently, but my intuition kept telling me otherwise. Something just did not feel right. As it turned out, the man who had raised me was not my father. Everyone but me knew. When the truth was revealed, my bonds were broken and trust disappeared. Meeting my new family was awkward. I felt like I didn't belong anywhere. With this one discovery, as a preteen, I lost my identity, my direction, and my voice. Until recently, I've rarely had a genuine conversation surrounding this with anyone. I shut down completely.

As a teen, I wanted to regain security and feel unconditional love. I became obsessed with creating my own family. I thought the life I wanted would come with a baby. By the age of nineteen, I was a single mom with a seventeen-month-old infant, confused and exhausted. We had been on a long wait list for low income housing and had recently been assigned to a unit in a new city, forty minutes from where we had been living. We were doing our best to settle into a new routine. I couldn't sleep, and yet every morning I had to get myself ready for school and get my son to the babysitter. I was juggling motherhood, school, work, and a possible career in figure skating. Having been a competitive skater growing up, it was a natural choice to coach or join an ice show, but then I would have to leave my baby behind. I couldn't decide which path to take until the day my life decided for me.

The morning of April 9, 2000 started easily. The previous night had been spent in a deep dream state. Everything was so vivid that I felt wide awake, and yet it was the best sleep I'd had since my son was born. I awoke refreshed, with a feeling that today something was different. We had an easy breakfast together and got dressed without fuss. My little boy was so cooperative. It started out as a perfect day.

We drove ninety minutes away to the ice rink that morning to find upon arrival that my practice had been cancelled. I gratefully headed home. Practice was too much commitment with everything else going on in my life. Ten minutes into the drive, everything shifted into slow motion as I remember looking back into the rearview mirror and feeling a sense of peace. I looked at my little boy and thought how perfect he was, what an angel. In those same few seconds, our car was hurtling end over end down the highway as my awareness hovered above. I wasn't afraid. In fact, it was a spiritual moment, devoid of panic, until I awoke to the sounds of emergency workers extracting me from the now-twisted heap of metal. All I could think was, "Where is my baby?"

By the time I was out of the car, a helicopter had air-lifted my baby to a nearby children's hospital. No one would tell me how he was and as I arrived by ambulance to the nearest hospital, I was prepared to expect the news of his possible death. My heart was torn and my mind conflicted over the quality of life he would have if he did survive. I have no memory of how I physically got to my son, though I'm almost certain it was a family member who took me to him. Of all days, this was the day my extended family was traveling from six hours away to gather at my aunt's house. The whole day was a huge series of synchronicities. The hospital my son had been taken to turned out to be within walking distance from our new apartment. For better or for worse, this was something that was meant to happen in our lives.

At first, there were a lot of people visiting, though I was in no state to receive them. For what felt like months, my son was in a coma and on life support. I did not leave the hospital until he was stable and moved onto a unit. During the days, I would tuck him into a little red wagon and walk laps around the building, pulling his IV pole along with us. I could not have felt lonelier or more lost. When I started to sleep at home, I'd wake up in a panic that something had happened and I'd rush to the hospital to find that nothing had changed. My energy would crash and we would resume our circling routine.

Months later, I brought home my miracle baby. I didn't know how to deal with my grief. Again, I held in my true feelings, not talking with anyone and functioning normally on the surface. I took up working nights in a nightclub and eventually hired a live-in nanny to help with his care. Her presence gave me the freedom to escape from my responsibilities. Being young and single and now accustomed to a pattern of an adrenaline rush followed by a crash made it easy to escape into a life of drugs and alcohol.

Working in nightclubs to earn money escalated my recreational drug use into a full-blown opiate and cocaine addiction. And still, I was so adept at pulling myself together that I was able to make people think I was fine. I was even stopped at several D.U.I. checkpoints in the early hours of the morning and released because I looked young, innocent, and did not fit the profile of someone living a harsh life in the fast lane. Every time I got away without even a reprimand, it gave me permission to push the envelope farther.

After several years of spinning out of control, I knew something needed to change. I felt guilty about not being present as a mother. I started reading self-help books. I didn't want to go out and party anymore. I just wanted to stay in my room, high on cocaine, and journal the nights away. I became brutally honest with myself, getting all of my feelings out on paper. The journaling helped me have a conscience and served the purpose of opening myself to everything I had been holding inside.

Moving to a new city was my solution to get away from my destructive lifestyle and start over. I went back to school, but because I didn't get help, I reverted to my old ways and got myself into trouble again. After one particularly crazy weekend, I was unable to pick up my son from his sitter because I was out doing drugs. I almost lost him for being an unfit mother. That's when I entered recovery.

I joined C.A., a twelve-step program for cocaine addiction. I immersed myself in a new lifestyle, attending daily meetings, sometimes two a day, and working the program. I went back to work at a nightclub because it was the only place I was comfortable making money. I stayed sober, but I was still a very lost as a person. The last thing I expected was a replacement addiction. I became bulimic, focusing all my attention on food to buy which I would later throw up. I switched to starving myself, then overeating, and back to extreme exercising, which gave me an adrenaline rush. My eating disorder became my new high as I simultaneously dove deeper into self-discovery.

I began to devote more and more time to changing my beliefs with support from personal development books and CD's. I was invited to a seminar to change my life at a cellular level and I found myself attending a retreat in Arizona. The three days of intensive, deep meditation and ceremonies helped me to release the dark past I had been carrying inside of me. I affirmed who I was in the moment and who I wanted to be. Surrounded by a healing community, I transformed into a new person from the inside out. When I came home, I collected every piece of my previous life into garbage bags and drove two hours to a nearby city to throw it away, in a place from which I would not be tempted to retrieve it. There was no going back now. This ritual anchored a visceral change in me, my mindset, and my career.

My passion for photography led me to create a sustainable photography business. I was hired to be a personal photographer for a well-known spiritual public figure, which enabled me to attend additional retreats around the world. When I'd come home from a trip, I would photograph local families. I was obsessed with baby photography and I also enjoyed helping women get comfortable in their own skin with boudoir shoots. I was talented, but I didn't know how to run a business. I was teaching myself, making a lot of mistakes, but I kept on going until I figured it out.

That day when I chose to throw everything from my past into the garbage, I had no clue what would happen next or how I would manage to start my new life. Opening my heart to receive love from others showed me how to love myself and find an abundance of the peace I yearned for. With the help of many others, I learned to be compassionate with myself, to connect with my spirit, and to get out of my own way so I can be truly who I am.

Intuition is of the greatest service in knowing the truth. It's how I lead my life. It's how I gauge relationships with everyone I meet and how I evaluate everything I do. It's not something I actively think about and as a child, I didn't know I was "doing it". Whenever I called someone out, I was told I was the liar. When I became a teenager, the lies of my childhood were revealed. Time confirmed what I had known all along. Even then, I didn't learn to trust myself until I got sober. The cleaner I live, the louder and more accurate my intuition has become.

Being in a peaceful place inside and around me is an important key to staying aligned with my higher purpose. By carving out time for spiritual practice, I attune to my true self and allow historical happenings to ease into the background. Some of the ways I do this may also be helpful for you. I teach this in my Abundant Woman program to help align people with their higher selves.

If an old experience reveals itself, trace it down and journal what originally happened. Follow the patterns to get to whatever the root experience is for you. It could be as a simple as a childhood memory of waiting for Dad to come home, but inside, the feeling is abandonment. Notice where else in your life you have felt this way. Take some time, as in meditation, to tell your younger self you are safe, and life will move past this moment. Share the wisdom of the adult you are now and how you got to this moment. Let go of any blame. Take your power back.

Biography

Carmell Pelly is the founder of The Abundant Woman, a program in which she speaks to other women about fully accepting themselves while trusting in the power of their higher callings without giving in to fear. Having tapped into her sensuality and femininity, Carmell has learned in such a way that it empowered her to create The Abundant Woman. As the mother of a teenager and new baby as well as being a wife, professional photographer, and successful entrepreneur, she has learned how to thrive by keeping herself aligned with her higher calling.

Carmell's journey to becoming an Abundant Woman was a turbulent path of self-discovery and learning. Through much wreckage and repair, Carmell has overcome many forms of abuse and addiction. Sober for almost 12 years, she has learned to love herself by exploring deep inside and finding out who she really is.

Today, as a feminine empowerment coach, Carmell has been able to explore her passions for travel, fashion, and health, helping women find and reconnect to their sensuality that leads to abundance. She helps bring out the soft, curvy, hidden side by looking at what is holding them back (such as fear, shame, or guilt). Through movement and photography, Carmell transforms the lives of woman worldwide.

Learn More...

www.theabundantwoman.ca

www.facebook.com/theabundantwoman/

www.instagram.com/theabundantwoman/

https://twitter.com/Carmell_Pelly